THE ATLAS of FLAGS

Illustrations by

ROSSELLA TRIONFETTI

Text by
FEDERICO SILVESTRI

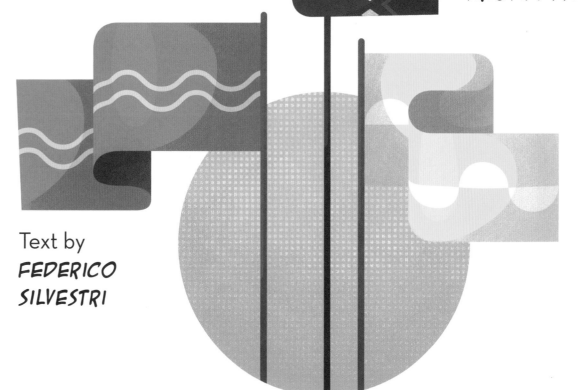

WHITE STAR KIDS

INTRODUCTION

At first glance, it would seem that a flag is nothing more than a SIMPLE RECTANGLE OF FABRIC with a design made of lines and colors—easy to reproduce and easy to recognize.

Well, a first impression has rarely been more MISTAKEN!

Every flag includes symbols and colors that recapitulate the HISTORY, the SENTIMENTS and the PRIDE of the citizens it represents.

But as you will see, flags are not unchangeable. Precisely because they represent a country's character and its strongest sentiments, they change along with the history of that country, which may, in some cases, have undergone a complete transformation over the centuries or decades or even in a matter of only a few years.

Knowing the flags of the world will allow you to KNOW THE SPIRIT OF A COUNTRY just as knowing the secret meanings hidden in your country's flag will TEACH YOU A LOT ABOUT YOUR OWN HISTORY AND CULTURE!

In the following pages, you will learn the language of flags as well as some curious facts and many secrets. . .

You will even learn the rules of flag design so YOU CAN MAKE ONE TO REPRESENT YOUR VERY OWN KINGDOM!

NORTH
AMERICA

ATLANTIC
OCEAN

CENTRAL
AMERICA

PACIFIC
OCEAN

SOUTH
AMERICA

CONTENTS

EUROPE

ASIA

PACIFIC
OCEAN

AFRICA

INDIAN
OCEAN

OCEANIA

HOW ARE FLAGS MADE?

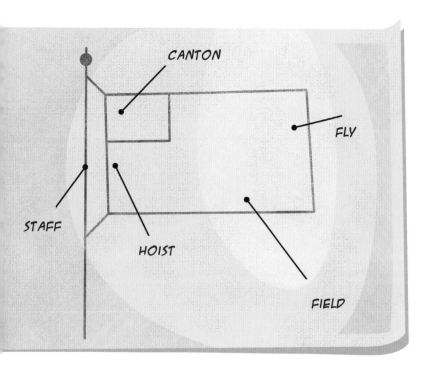

CANTON

FLY

STAFF

HOIST

FIELD

CANTONS, INCLEMENT WEATHER AND SIMPLICITY

The answer might seem obvious at first. After all, what is a flag but a simple rectangular piece of cloth?

First of all, not every part of the flag is the same and some are more important than others.

The **canton**, the most important part of the flag, is the place of honor. It is where you will find the flag's most representative features.

The canton is usually the upper left quarter of the flag near the **hoist** side, where it is sewn, or inserted through a sheath, the rope with which the flag is anchored to the pole, or **staff**. The background of the flag is called the **field** and the right side—the farthest away from the staff—is the **fly**.

The fly is the part most exposed to the wind and the inclement weather, so it is more easily damaged than the hoist side, usually better preserved. That is why the canton is on the left side—it would not make any sense to put the most important elements on the side that might end up all frayed. Of course, a flag should never be allowed to deteriorate too much and should always be substituted before that happens. But sometimes that is not possible: just think about ships on a long voyage.

That is why a flag has to be designed with the elements in mind; it will always be out there flying, rain or shine, in the wind and at the mercy of all kinds of adverse weather conditions.

Often, the center of the flag is also a position for significant elements but there are a lot of strange exceptions and the flag of Zambia is one of them. The flag's distinctive elements, an eagle and three colored stripes, are all on the right. It seems like Zambia likes to be original, at least as far as its flag goes.

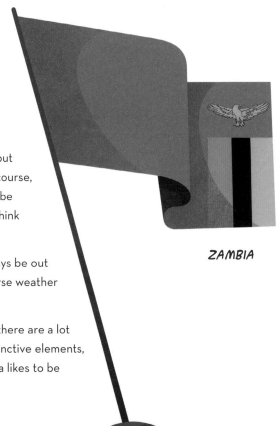

ZAMBIA

SWITZERLAND

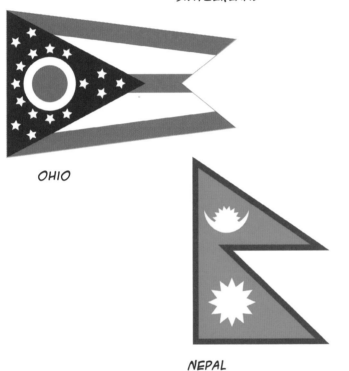

OHIO

Flags can have many different shapes. Some are square or dovetail and some are odd triangular shapes, but the vast majority are rectangular.

Flags come in a variety of proportions as well. The long side might even be twice as long as the short side or there may be no proportion at all in their lengths.

The sides of the flag of Togo respect the proportions of golden ratio, which for centuries were considered the best proportions for a rectangle. Of course, that makes it a little difficult to produce since with a short side of 1 meter (which corresponds to 3.3 feet), the long side has to be 1 meter and 61,803398875 cm —more or less, because the decimals go on infinitely but the Togolese have decided that it is close enough.

All right, now I am ready to draw a flag of my own. My yard is a big (well, sort of) new country and I am the president or even the king. So I need a flag that is recognizable and hopefully beautiful, too.

NAVA, the North American Vexillological Association, published a useful book called *Good Flag, Bad Flag* where you will find five simple rules (plus an unwritten sixth rule) that are guidelines written to help people like us, who want to design a new flag.

NEPAL

JAMAICA

KEEP IT SIMPLE

A flag that is easy to draw is easy to remember. Actually, a flag should be simple enough for a child to draw, so that children all over can try their hand. Besides, a simple flag on a faraway ship is easier to recognize and that helps to avoid any unnecessary confusion.

This is the flag of Jamaica. It is very simple and easy to recognize and it leaves a lasting impression. You will find it on just about anything that comes from Jamaica.

USE MEANINGFUL SYMBOLS

Every flag has its meaning and symbolism. It conveys a message
or describes the nation it represents, so the symbols on it should be
meaningful and not just something we choose because we like it
or because everyone else is using it.

CANADA

This is the flag of Canada.
It has a simple design and a clear layout. The maple leaf
at its center is certainly a Canadian symbol—Canadians
love the maple syrup that they drizzle on their pancakes.
They even have a holiday to celebrate it.

DO NOT USE TOO MANY COLORS

Using a lot of colors might sound like a good idea but too many colors make flags
too complicated and hard to identify. Besides, having to find a lot of colors makes
a flag more difficult to reproduce and that was a problem in the past.

But above all remember this: with only two or three colors, it is easier to find
a combination of colors that contrast well and do not blend into one another.

ESTONIA

The flag of the little country
of Estonia uses three colors that
contrast well and are reminiscent
of the snow, the dark pine forests,
and the sky.

NO WRITING

Writing is hard to read at a distance, so it is not very useful on a flag. Currently, there are no flags
of any sovereign states with writing on them, except for some tiny inscriptions on certain coats of arms.
Luckily, the designers of the most important flags know this rule well.

Still, some American cities and states seem to have a passion for writing on their flags.

DISTINGUISH YOURSELF FROM THE OTHERS OR SHOW YOUR TIES TO THEM

If you want to be recognizable, you need to stand out from the crowd. You need to find a way to distinguish yourself from other countries. Greece's flag is a good example: it is hard to find a similar flag. But sometimes it is more appropriate to show the ties you have to other countries or regions—whether they be cultural, religious, political, or geographical.

In fact, entire families of flags exist. They have symbols and colors in common and they unite countries that share the same ties.

GREECE

One of the most famous families of flags is that of the Scandinavian cross: it is an off-centered Christian cross. All of the Nordic countries use this design and when their flags fly together, the effect is powerful indeed.

BREAKING THE RULES

All rules get broken sooner or later. And as a matter of fact there are many flags that violate one or more of these rules: perhaps they have five colors, or an unusual shape, or a symbol that is truly difficult to draw—but they are all, nevertheless, beautiful and much loved by their citizens.

The flag of South Africa is a great example of a flag that is full of colors and features an unusual design. Each of its colors carries a very precise meaning!

It is better not to write anything on your flag but if you must break the rule, do it in a very subtle and careful way.

This is the case of the state flag of Colorado. Its initial has been transformed into a glowing sun that looks like it is shining in the Colorado Desert.

So, those are the rules: our flag should be simple, with only a few contrasting colors and meaningful symbols, there should be no writing, and it can either be unique or tied to a family of flags. An easy way to start designing your own flag is to begin by drawing on a sheet of paper the size of an index card. That way, you can see what the flag will look like at a distance and avoid making important mistakes.

SOUTH AFRICA

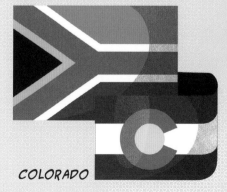

COLORADO

RECORDS

Every flag has its own story and meaning. Some also have an extra card to play.

THE OLDEST

Let us start with when the first flag in the world was invented. The Roman Empire used objects that were similar to flags to identify their legions and, once they came into contact with Sarmatian warriors, adopted their Draconarius. Other empires, too, like the Sasanian Empire, used some kind of insignia to identify various parts of their armies—but all of these examples pale in comparison to the banner of Shahdad.

This flag is truly special—according to archeologists, it is around 5,000 years old! How did such an old flag survive until today? Simple—it is made of bronze!

In order to understand which flag is the oldest in the world, we need to look at both history and ancient beliefs, like legends and stories. According to one legend, the origins of the flag of Austria date back to 1191, the year the Battle of Acre was fought. After the battle, Duke Leopold of Austria found his tunic soiled with blood and, taking off his sword belt, revealed a single white stripe of cloth that was still clean. This is the origin of the Austrian flag—a bit of a gruesome story, perhaps, but then again, the dukes and leaders of the ancient world were not known for their subtlety.

According to another legend, the flag of Scotland is even older, and its origins even more obscure, dating all the way back to 830 A.D. On the night before the battle between the Picts and the Angles, Oengus II, king of the Picts, dreamt of St. Andrew assuring him that he would win the upcoming battle. The next day, Oengus saw the shape of the cross of St. Andrew in the clouds, and—who knows whether by coincidence or not—emerged victorious in battle. What is certain is that the image, perhaps first spotted in the form of clouds against the blue background of the sky, is now fixed upon the Scottish flag.

Lastly, the flag that has been used for the longest time by a sovereign state is the flag of Denmark, nicknamed "Danneborg." Various legends recounting its origin all agree on one fact: that the flag had, literally, fallen from the sky.

AUSTRIA

SCOTLAND

THE BANNER
OF SHAHDAD

THE YOUNGEST

After struggling to find the oldest flag, finding the youngest flag is much easier.

It is the flag of South Sudan, which only became independent in 2011. Although it is still quite young, the design originated earlier—in the 1980's, when it was used by the factions that were fighting for independence.

Its colors bring to mind the Pan-African flag, which is red, black and green, but with the addition of the color blue, which represents the waters of the Nile River that crosses the country.

SOUTH SUDAN

THE SHORTEST LIFE

Flags, like countries, do not always last forever. Some nations or governments last for a short time —some for a few days, others just for a few hours.

Many countries, of course, use pre-existing flags, like the kingdoms of the Persian Gulf that enjoyed independence for just a single day before uniting to form the United Arab Emirates, or the Republic of Crimea, which uses the same flag that it had before it declared its secession from Ukraine.

The title for the flag with the shortest life goes to the flag of the Republic of Benin, a state that lasted from the morning of September 19, 1967, until lunchtime of the next day, when the Nigerian forces overtook the region once and for all.

DENMARK

BENIN

THE FARTHEST AWAY

Contrary to what you might think, the flag farthest away from the planet is not the one famously planted on the moon by American astronauts during the Apollo 11 mission. Actually, the flag farthest away is currently onboard the spacecraft Voyager 1 that, in its journey into deep space, is the most distant object from Earth.

This means there is a little American flag more than 12 billion miles from Earth! To give us a better idea, if our sun were the size of a grape, the Voyager and the flag aboard it would be almost 330 yards away from it.

FAMILIES OF FLAGS

COLORS, SYMBOLS AND DESIGNS

As we have seen in the rules devoted to flag design, it is important that countries use their flag to show their ties to other nations.

There are many groups of flags that share common designs, colors or symbols. Each of them tells you something about their culture and history as a nation, even if you have never heard of the country before. We will tell you more about the ideas behind each family of flags and give you some examples.

PAN-ARABIC COLORS

THE COLORS OF THE UPRISING

Pan-Arabic colors are the ones frequently used on the flags of the Arab states. These colors were united for the first time during the Arab revolt against the Ottoman Empire. Each color symbolizes a dynasty or an era of the Arab culture. The black was used by Muhammed, the white by the Umayyad caliphate, the green by the Fatimids, and the red by the Hashemites and the Husseins.

But the flag of the Arab insurrection was designed by an Englishman, Sir Mark Sykes, in an attempt to create a symbol that would unite the Arabs in the war. His gesture may not have been totally disinterested since he wrote a secret agreement, along with the Frenchman Picot, to define the areas of influence once they were free from Ottoman control.

From the 1950's to the present day, many nations have adopted these colors, which have become a symbol of pride and union.

Except for the green, these colors are also used in the Egyptian version which was inspired by the 1916 revolt as well.

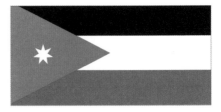

JORDAN

IRAQ

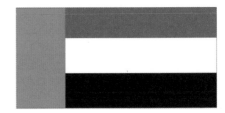

UNITED ARAB EMIRATES

SYRIA

EGYPT

GHANA

MALAWI

REPUBLIC
OF THE CONGO

TOGO

GUINEA-BISSAU

PAN-AFRICAN COLORS

THE COLORS OF INDEPENDENCE

The term "Pan-African" is composed of two words: "Pan", which means "all", and "African", whose meaning is quite obvious. The word indicates something that unites all—or most—of the countries of that continent. Let us keep in mind the word "Pan" as it will be a frequently recurring theme in this part of the book.

There are two color combinations that are considered Pan-African: yellow, red and green, inspired by the traditional flag of Ethiopia, and black, red and green, chosen by the UNIA—a black national organization founded in Jamaica by Marcus Garvey. His goal among others was the return of the slaves' descendants from the United States to Liberia, Africa.

To this day there are many countries that adopt these color combinations. The colors of Ethiopia were chosen because, apart from a brief period of Italian occupation, this country was the only one to escape the colonial powers of Europe, arousing admiration and thus becoming an example for many African nations.

Here are some examples of African flags that use variations of these two color combinations. Ghana and Guinea-Bissau use all four colors with an intelligent placement of the black star, a symbol of fraternity. Togo, on the other hand, uses a combination of the stars and stripes pattern and the Ethiopian colors.

COLOMBIAN COLORS

PAN-SLAVIC COLORS

CENTRAL AMERICAN COLORS

THE STAR AND CRESCENT

FROM MESOPOTAMIA TO TODAY

The star and crescent that accompanies it are a widely used symbol in Islamic nations. They can be found in many national flags from West Africa to the eastern end of the Indian Ocean in Malaysia.

The design was adopted for the first time by the Ottoman Empire during the 18th century and spread throughout the period of its greatest expansion.

MALDIVES

ALGERIA

MAURITANIA

The Ottomans borrowed the star and crescent (crescent is a waxing moon) from the Byzantines but the symbol actually has much older origins that can be traced to the Sumerian civilization in Mesopotamia. It was a very popular symbol. The Egyptians used it to write the word "month", and it can be also found on the border stones used by the Babylonians.

The star initially represented the planet Venus, also known as the "morning star" but in later times it was also associated with the sun.

On most of today's flags, the tips of the crescent moon point to the right as they did on the Ottoman (and Turkish) version, but there are some exceptions such as Mauritania. Sometimes, the crescent is not accompanied by the star, as is the case with the Maldives.

THE SCANDINAVIAN CROSS

FALLEN FROM THE SKY

When you see a Scandinavian cross, or Nordic cross, you immediately think of Northern Europe. This design was introduced by Denmark and there is evidence that the unmistakable asymmetric design of the Scandinavian Cross dates back to the 18th century, but it is probably much older. A popular legend narrates that it fell directly from the sky a long time ago in 1219. Unfortunately, we will never know the name of the person who designed it but we do know for sure that the Nordic Cross is a Christian symbol!

Its conquests and alliances with other Northern States such as Sweden and Norway made Denmark a very influential nation in Northern Europe and its flag inspired the flags of the entire region. The Nordic Cross can be found on the flags of five independent countries but its popularity is much more far reaching. You can find it in the provinces of the Netherlands, in Russia and beyond. One of its most recent appearances is on the flag of South Uist Island in Scotland.

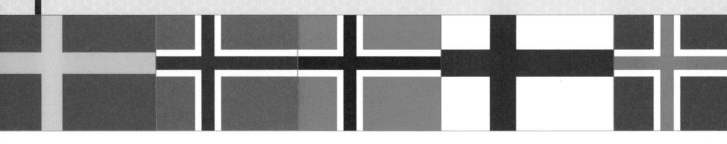

SWEDEN   **SOUTH UIST**   **NORWAY**   **FINLAND**   **ICELAND**

THE SOUTHERN CROSS

PRACTICALLY A COMPASS

If you find a flag with this symbol on it as you are travelling around the world, you can be almost certain that you are in the Southern Hemisphere. That information might seem a little vague but you have to start somewhere.

Just as the North Star can be used to get your bearings in the Northern Hemisphere, the Southern Cross helps to determine which direction is south in the Southern Hemisphere.

It is one of the brightest constellations in the sky, and it is visible all year long.

In a hemisphere far less populated than the Northern one, many nations of the Southern Hemisphere use the Southern Cross on their flags to indicate their geographic position.

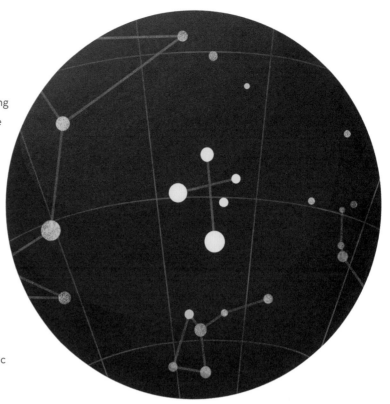

AUSTRALIA

TIERRA DEL FUEGO PROVINCE, ARGENTINA

SAMOAN ISLANDS

CHRISTMAS ISLAND

PAPUA NEW GUINEA

The Southern Cross was first used during the Eureka rebellion in Australia when the miners of Ballarat rose up against the powers of the United Kingdom. It was quite different than the one in use today.

The stars of the Southern Cross are usually depicted on a blue or black background representing the sky and they can be also found in many regional flags. The cross holds the place of honor, the canton, on the Samoan Islands flag and can be found together with the countries' national birds on the flags of Papua New Guinea, Christmas Island and Fire Land. The flags of Australia and New Zealand are good examples too.

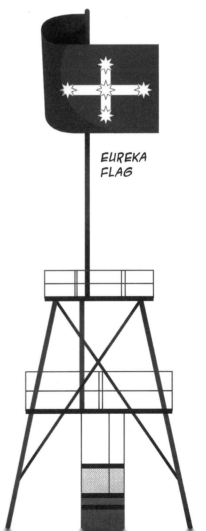

EUREKA FLAG

HIDDEN MAPS

GEOGRAPHICAL FLAGS

BOSNIA-HERZEGOVINA

At first glance, these flags might seem like any other, but a careful observer will see that they are actually little maps.

Whoever drew these flags knew how to secretly incorporate a stylized drawing of the country, region or city that the flag represented into the design and still keep it simple and elegant.

In Europe, Bosnia-Herzegovina's flag is a good example of this kind of flag—it represents the country's general geographical shape. The flag was adopted a few years after the country's independence in an attempt to create a symbol that would not be associated with the recent war. The country, in fact, experienced an ugly civil war between 1992 and 1995, the year the Dayton agreement was signed to mark the end of the conflict. The triangle represents Bosnia-Herzegovina and symbolizes the three principal ethnic groups of the country: Croatians, Bosnians and Serbs. Its colors—blue, white and yellow—are associated with peace and neutrality and have a strong European connection.

Another excellent example is the flag of the small state of Nauru, the third smallest country in the world: a tropical island of just 8.1 square miles and a little over ten thousand inhabitants.

It is located in the Pacific Ocean, at just 35 miles from the equator, the line that divides the Earth into two equal parts.

NAURU

You can easily imagine what the flag's elements represent: the blue background is the Pacific Ocean, the yellow line is the equator and the white, twelve-point star is the Island of Nauru itself.

KAGOSHIMA

The flags of the prefectures in Japan are a perfect example of effective and essential design. They almost all follow the common theme of a central monochromatic symbol. The central symbols are often Japanese letters, flowers, plants or stylized animals. Some prefectures however, have chosen to represent the map of their territory in the synthetic, essential style of these flags.

One of these is Kagoshima. The map on the flag is very stylized but the large bay of Kagoshima and Mount Sakurajima, the great volcano colored in red, are still very recognizable.

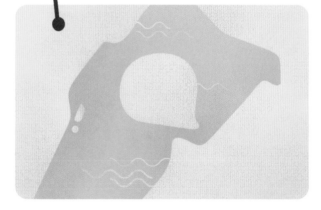

The small state of Saint Lucia is one of the many counties that make up the Lesser Antilles in the Caribbean Sea. Its map is different than the prevoius ones, but it does a good job of representing the island just the same. The blue background is the crystalline Caribbean Sea and the two overlapping triangles represent one of the island's most important symbols: the two peaks of Saint Lucia—its twin volcanoes, Gros Piton and Petit Piton.

The flag of the city of Madison, Wisconsin in the United States is also interesting. The city is located on an isthmus, a small strip of land between two lakes. Madison is also the capitol of Wisconsin and like most capitals, has a Capital Building, seat of the government, which in this case is located in the center of the isthmus.

MADISON

Looking at the flag and a map, it is easy to understand the symbolism of the design. It is a fairly accurate drawing of the shape of the city: the blue represents the two lakes, the white is the isthmus and the cross in the middle is the same shape as the Capitol Building.

SAINT LUCIA

ALL THE FLAGS OF THE WORLD

Here they are: 197 official and recognized national flags! As we have seen, most are rectangular, but try to identify the flags that deviate from this tradition, choosing square shapes, like Switzerland for example, or completely unusual outlines, like the extraordinary flag of Nepal. Some of them are very simple, others very complicated and use strange symbols and bold color combinations. One glance is enough to understand that each of them hides unique meanings, stories and symbols.

EUROPE

 ICELAND

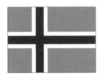 NORWAY

 SWEDEN

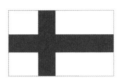 FINLAND

 IRELAND

 UNITED KINGDOM

 PORTUGAL

 SPAIN

 ANDORRA

 FRANCE

 MONACO

 LUXEMBOURG

 BELGIUM

 THE NETHERLANDS

 GERMANY

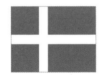 DENMARK

 SWITZERLAND

 LIECHTENSTEIN

 AUSTRIA

 ITALY

 SAN MARINO

 VATICAN CITY

 MALTA

 SLOVENIA

 CROATIA

 BOSNIA-HERZEGOVINA

 SERBIA

 MONTENEGRO

 KOSOVO

 ALBANIA

 MACEDONIA

 GREECE

 CYPRUS

 BULGARIA

 ROMANIA

 HUNGARY

 SLOVAKIA

 CZECH REPUBLIC

 POLAND

 LITHUANIA

 LATVIA

 ESTONIA

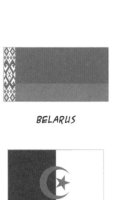 BELARUS

 UKRAINE

 MOLDAVIA

 RUSSIA

 MOROCCO

 ALGERIA

 TUNISIA

 LIBYA

 EGYPT

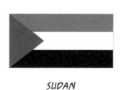 SUDAN

 CHAD

 NIGER

 MALI

 MAURITANIA

 CAPE VERDE

 SENEGAL

 THE GAMBIA

 GUINEA-BISSAU

 GUINEA

 SIERRA LEONE

 LIBERIA

 IVORY COAST

 BURKINA FASO

 GHANA

 TOGO

 BENIN

 NIGERIA

 CAMEROON

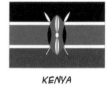 CENTRAL AFRICAN REPUBLIC

 SOUTH SUDAN

 ETHIOPIA

 ERITREA

 DJIBOUTI

 SOMALIA

 KENYA

 TANZANIA

 UGANDA

 RWANDA

 BURUNDI

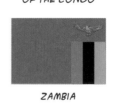 DEM. REPUBLIC OF THE CONGO

 REPUBLIC OF THE CONGO

 GABON

 EQUATORIAL GUINEA

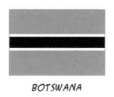 SÃO TOMÉ AND PRÍNCIPE

 ANGOLA

 ZAMBIA

 MALAWI

MOZAMBIQUE

ZIMBABWE

BOTSWANA

NAMIBIA

SOUTH AFRICA

LESOTHO

19

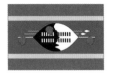 SWAZILAND

 MADAGASCAR

 MAURITIUS

 COMOROS

 SEYCHELLES

ASIA

 TURKEY

 ARMENIA

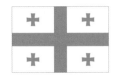 GEORGIA

 AZERBAIJAN

 SYRIA

 LEBANON

 ISRAEL

 PALESTINIAN TERRITORIES

 JORDAN

 SAUDI ARABIA

 YEMEN

 OMAN

 UNITED ARAB EMIRATES

 QATAR

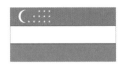 BAHRAIN

 KUWAIT

 IRAQ

 IRAN

 AFGHANISTAN

 TURKMENISTAN

 UZBEKISTAN

 KAZAKHSTAN

 KYRGYZSTAN

 TAJIKISTAN

 PAKISTAN

 INDIA

 SRI LANKA

 MALDIVES

 NEPAL

 BHUTAN

 BANGLADESH

 MYANMAR

 THAILAND

 MALAYSIA

 SINGAPORE

 LAOS

 CAMBODIA

 VIETNAM

 PEOPLE'S REPUBLIC OF CHINA

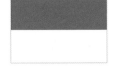 MONGOLIA

 NORTH KOREA

 SOUTH KOREA

 JAPAN

 PHILIPPINES

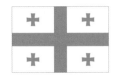 BRUNEI

 INDONESIA

 EAST TIMOR

OCEANIA

PALAU

PAPUA
NEW GUINEA

SOLOMON ISLANDS

AUSTRALIA

NEW ZEALAND

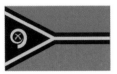
VANUATU

FIJI

TONGA

COOK ISLANDS

SAMOA

TUVALU

NAURU

FEDERATED STATES
OF MICRONESIA

MARSHALL ISLANDS

KIRIBATI

NORTH AND CENTRAL AMERICA

CANADA

UNITED STATES
OF AMERICA

MEXICO

BELIZE

GUATEMALA

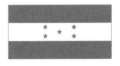
HONDURAS

EL SALVADOR

NICARAGUA

COSTA RICA

PANAMA

BAHAMAS

CUBA

HAITI

DOMINICAN REPUBLIC

JAMAICA

SAINT KITTS
AND NEVIS

ANTIGUA
AND BARBUDA

DOMINICA

SAINT LUCIA

SAINT VINCENT
AND THE GRENADINES

BARBADOS

GRENADA

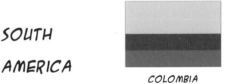
TRINIDAD
AND TOBAGO

SOUTH AMERICA

COLOMBIA

VENEZUELA

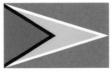
GUYANA

SURINAME

BRAZIL

ECUADOR

PERU

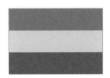
BOLIVIA

PARAGUAY

URUGUAY

ARGENTINA

CHILE

EUROPE

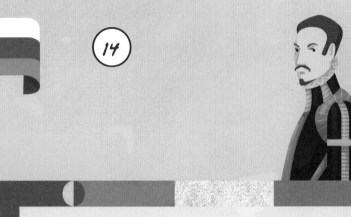

⑭

SPAIN

The Spanish flag is made up of three stripes—red, yellow and red—with a coat of arms placed not at the center, but in one of the thirds of the fly.

Without a doubt, the most interesting and rich part of the flag is its coat of arms, which is a true synthesis of Spanish history.

Heraldry, the discipline that studies coats of arms, uses a very complex and technical language to describe the characteristics of armory. It is very precisely but here we will use a simpler and more straightforward language—let us think of it as our first dive into the world of heraldry.

In the coat of arms, there are the arms, or symbols, of the kingdoms that went on to form current Spain. There is Castile, "The Land of Castles," represented by a castle with three towers; León, depicted by its lion in purple; Aragon, portrayed by its famous historic motif of gold and red stripes called pallets; Navarre, symbolized by a golden chain with an emerald in the middle (this chain is supposed to have guarded the Moorish king during the Reconquista and was cut to pieces by the sword of Sancho VII of Navarre); and finally, the kingdom of Granada, characterized by a pomegranate.

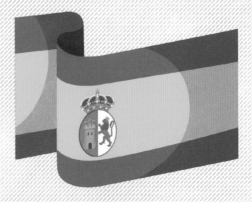

The columns that support the coat of arms are called the Pillars of Hercules, which was an ancient name given to the Strait of Gibraltar, and represent the strait today. Its motto *Plus Ultra*, or "Further Beyond," refers to the fact that, for centuries, the strait represented the limit of the ancient world, at least for the people of the Mediterranean.

The two columns are topped with an imperial crown to the right and a royal crown to the left, while the coat of arms is topped with the Spanish Royal crown. Finally, the tiny coat of arms at the very center depicts the fleur-de-lis of the royal Bourbon-Anjou family.

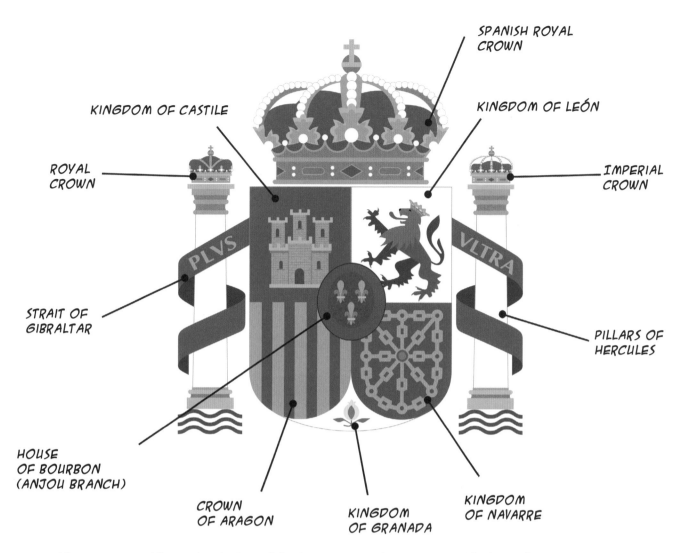

SPANISH ROYAL CROWN

KINGDOM OF LEÓN

KINGDOM OF CASTILE

ROYAL CROWN

IMPERIAL CROWN

PLVS

VLTRA

STRAIT OF GIBRALTAR

PILLARS OF HERCULES

HOUSE OF BOURBON (ANJOU BRANCH)

CROWN OF ARAGON

KINGDOM OF GRANADA

KINGDOM OF NAVARRE

Like many national flags today, the Spanish flag began as a naval ensign. In 1785, Charles III of Spain was given twelve different designs, and chose one quite similar to the flag we see today. It was red and yellow—colors traditionally associated with Aragon, Castile and Navarre—and featured a coat of arms in the center, with the symbols of Castile and León.

From then on, all Spanish flags would become variations of this same design, and only change depending on the government in power at that time.

The Spanish Republic, which was opposed to and overthrew the ancient monarchy, modified the flag so that the bottommost stripe was purple, or *morado*. This Republican flag ceased to exist in 1939, but it has been adopted at times by various political movements.

With the advent of dictator Francisco Franco, the flag returned to a design that much resembled its prior version, but with the addition of a complex coat of arms depicting an eagle, a symbol of St. John the Evangelist.

PORTUGAL

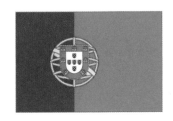

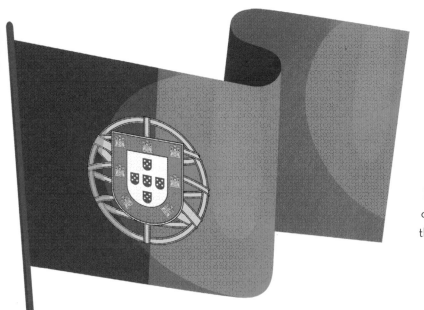

The Portuguese flag is made up of two colors: green and red, with a simplified national coat of arms, featuring an armillary sphere and Portuguese shield, at the center.

The armillary sphere, also known as a spherical astrolabe, is an ancient instrument used to model objects in space. It is associated with the age of discovery and navigation when the Portuguese became known for discovering new lands, founding colonies and maintaining trading posts throughout the world.

But red and green are not traditional Portuguese colors. In fact, before the Portuguese Republic was established in 1910, its colors were white and blue. These were the colors of the old flag that also featured the Portuguese shield, but without the armillary sphere.

The decision to change its colors was controversial: after rejecting the idea of a red, revolutionary flag, the country chose both red and green, colors that recalled the banner hoisted on the *Adamastor*, one of the rebel ships that first gave the signal of revolt.

The original flag of the *Adamastor* used green and red, because they were colors associated with the Republican faction. With the later Republican victory, green and red became its official colors.

Besides being blue and white, the old flag was not asymmetrical while the naval flag had the same design that we see on the Portuguese flag today.

ASTROLABE

VERSION UNTIL 1910

26

GREECE

The flag of Greece is composed of nine horizontal blue and white stripes with a white cross on a blue background as its canton.

The cross is a homage to the Greek Orthodox Church, the social and cultural glue during the Ottoman rule that lasted for three centuries. The nine stripes represent the nine syllables of the motto of independence *Eleutheria i Thanathos*, which meant "Freedom or Death"—a motto used by Greeks in support of independence during the rebellions against the Ottoman Turks.

The Greek Revolution erupted in 1821, during which they used a flag with a blue cross on a white background, a motif dating back to the 18th century.

After a decade of war, both the Turks and foreign powers acknowledged Greek independence, but imposed the establishment of a monarchy. The German Prince Otto of Bavaria was chosen to rule until he was eventually deposed in 1862. Because of this, a common explanation for the color choice of the Greek flag is that they were borrowed from those of the Bavarian flag. A more popular theory states that the colors simply remind others of the sky and sea of Greece.

1821 REVOLUTIONARY FLAG

Today's flag made its first appearance as a naval flag, while the ensign of the state was, for a long time, merely a simple cross on a blue background.

The naval flag, though, eventually became so popular that it became the national flag. The flag, extremely popular among Greek citizens, is called *Kianolefki* or *Galanolefki*, which means "Blue-White" or "Sky-Blue-White."

The exact shade of blue is not precisely defined due to some ambiguity in the law that regulates the design of the flag, so that the final color is up to the discretion of those who manufacture the flag—but in any case, the differences, if any, are minimal.

NAVAL FLAG

ΕΛΕΥΘΕΡΙΑ
Η
ΘΑΝΑΤΟΣ

During the dictatorship of the Regime of the Colonels, the shade of blue used for the flag was noticeably darker, almost becoming a midnight blue instead. With the reinstatement of democracy, the Greek flag brought back its paler and softer blue.

ITALY

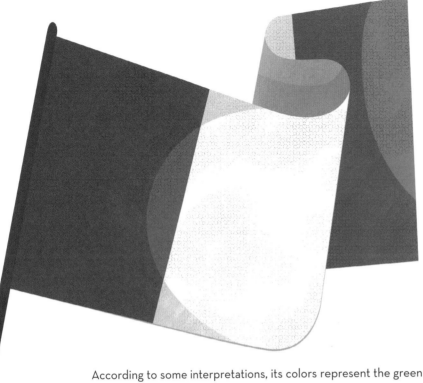

The Italian flag is an example of the European tricolor flag, which was created during the turbulent period of revolution that led to the Jacobin Republic, formed after a wave of idealism from the French Revolution.

According to some interpretations, its colors represent the green of the hills, the white of the snowy Alps, and the blood shed by the Italian revolutionaries and independents. Another version connects the colors to three religious values: hope, faith, and charity. The subversive nature of the flag when it was initially created in the late 18th century is evidence that this meaning was added later.

The flag of Italy is older than the country itself, which was united only in 1861. The first flag with these Italian colors dates back to the Cispadane Republic, which was formed in 1796 by combining the regions of Reggio Emilia, Bologna, Modena, and Ferrara.

The green color distinguishes the Italian flag from the French flag. It is symbolic of the green and white uniform of the Civic Guard of Milan, which was established in 1782 and was active during Austria's reign over the Lombardy region in Italy. The red of the Italian flag comes from the red and white of the flag of Milan.

KINGDOM OF ITALY

28

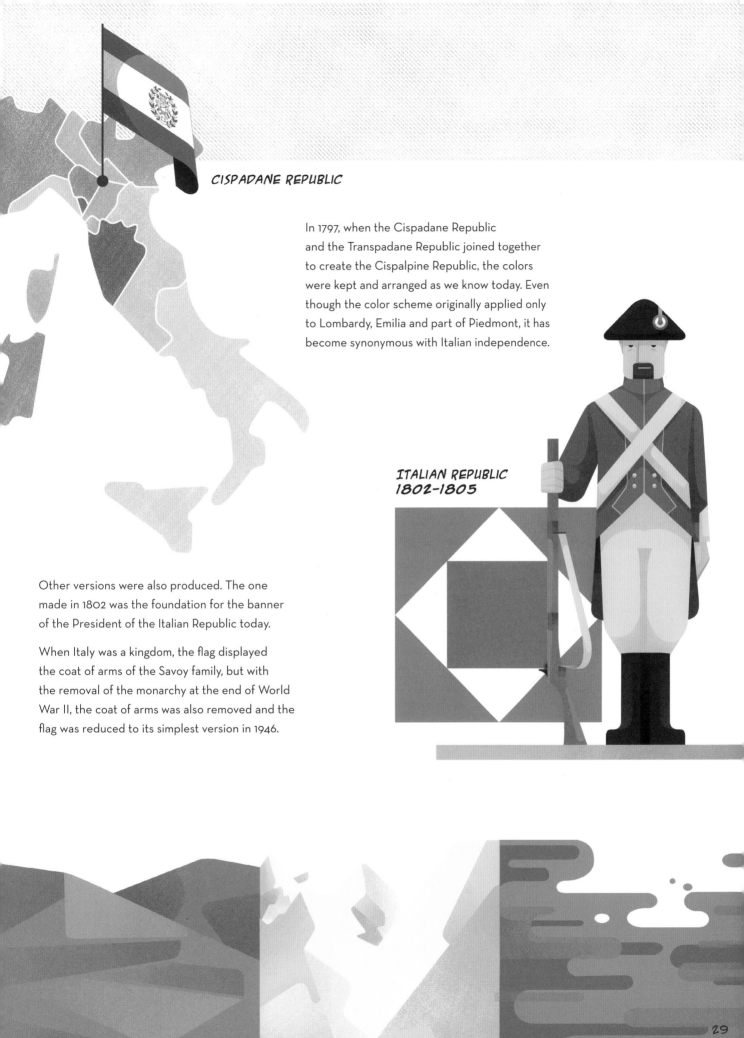

CISPADANE REPUBLIC

In 1797, when the Cispadane Republic and the Transpadane Republic joined together to create the Cispalpine Republic, the colors were kept and arranged as we know today. Even though the color scheme originally applied only to Lombardy, Emilia and part of Piedmont, it has become synonymous with Italian independence.

ITALIAN REPUBLIC 1802-1805

Other versions were also produced. The one made in 1802 was the foundation for the banner of the President of the Italian Republic today.

When Italy was a kingdom, the flag displayed the coat of arms of the Savoy family, but with the removal of the monarchy at the end of World War II, the coat of arms was also removed and the flag was reduced to its simplest version in 1946.

FRANCE

The French flag is the classic tricolor. A tricolor flag is made up of three vertical bands of equal size but of different colors and is usually associated with the ideals of an independent republic. The first tricolor was the Dutch flag, although it was split horizontally rather than vertically.

As a matter of fact, France does not just have any tricolor flag. Its flag has become a model for other European countries, as well as for countries all over the world. This is because, during the French Revolution, France supported many other nations in revolting against their own monarchies of the period.

In fact, the Italian flag gets its appearance from this era even though, at the time, it was technically the Cisalpine Republic, which was in northern Italy.

The design with vertical stripes was radically new for its time and was born out of a moment of revolution and chaos.

There is a beautiful painting by Leon Cogniet that depicts the turbulent origins of the flag. It shows the old, white cloth of the monarchy—partly stained with red blood from the revolution on one side and ripped on the other side, allowing a glimpse of the blue sky. Here, the three colors together create the French tricolor.

What do the colors represent? One widespread belief says that they represent the Revolutionary concepts of: Liberty, Equality and Fraternity. In reality, white was the color of the old monarchy, while red and blue were the colors that the city of Paris adopted from the first soldiers who took over the Bastille.

We all know that the French are a population of artists and, in fact, their flag appears in a great number of artworks; sometimes it is the central character as in the case of our Cogniet painting.

TOGO

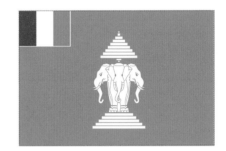

LAOS

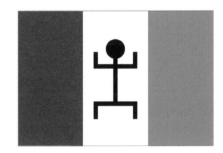

FRENCH SUDAN

In *Liberty Leading the People* by Eugene Delacroix, the main figure is the revolutionary flag. Those who are extra-attentive (and equipped with excellent vision) will see a second, miniscule, flag waved by one of the revolutionaries. The flag also appears in other more cheerful paintings, like *The Rue Montorgueil in Paris (Celebration of June 30, 1878)* by Claude Monet. Here, a street in Paris is completely flooded in blue, white and red in celebration of a national holiday.

In addition to having inspired many flags like the ones of Italy, Ireland and Romania, France has also produced many flags for its previous colonies—always with the French tricolor in the place of honor, the canton, of course.

Some examples are the flags of its ex-colonies: Togo, Laos, and the French Sudan (or what is known today as Mali).

We can also see this kind of flag in territories still under French control, like the French Southern and Antarctic Lands (abbreviated as TAAF, for Terres Australes et Antarctiques Françaises), or in regions that are culturally very close to France, like Acadia.

TAAF

ACADIA

UNITED KINGDOM

The flag of the United Kingdom, nicknamed the "Union Jack", is one of the most famous and most well-known flags of the world. It is both cleverly designed and complicated and is one of the most successful examples of combining different flags. It is a symbol that is as much loved as it is disputed by its citizens, given the amount of history, symbolism, and identity that is wrapped up in the flag.

Like its name suggests, the United Kingdom is made up of various political and cultural entities: England, Scotland, Wales, and Northern Ireland. Along with these are also a myriad of territories that enjoy special status such as Mann Island, Gibraltar, the Channel Islands, and a number of dependent territories overseas, left over from the British Empire.

The flag is made up of layered crosses: the cross of St. George, representing England, the cross of St. Andrew, depicting Scotland, and the cross of St. Patrick, portraying Northern Ireland. The English cross of St. George, with a red and white border, can be found in the foreground as the topmost layer, superimposed over the Irish cross of St. Patrick, which also has a red and white border, and the Scottish cross (nicknamed the Saltire), which provides the blue background of the flag. The blue of Union Jack, though, is a darker shade than the original Scottish blue color.

As you can see in the illustration, the Union Jack is not symmetrical. The Irish and Scottish crosses are designed to be on the same level: indeed, each diagonal arm is divided between the cross of St. Andrew and the cross of St. Patrick, so that Scottish representation is not relegated to a simple border. In each quarter of the Union Jack, Ireland and Scotland alternately occupy the upper position.

But what about Wales? There is no element in the flag that represents the nation of Wales. In 1606, when James VI of Scotland (who later became James I of England) decreed that a new flag be created to commemorate the union between the kingdoms of Scotland and England, Wales was still part of the kingdom of England and so, it was indirectly represented by the English cross. James VI of Scotland was also responsible for the name we have for the flag; Jack, in fact, is a shortening of Jacobus, the Latin version of James.

Whether it was the relative position of the cross or the lack of a symbol from Wales, the flag has attracted several proposals for revisions. The Scottish designed, and occasionally used, a Union Jack flag with the cross of St. Andrew as the uppermost layer, while in Parliament, there was a proposal to add the red dragon of Wales to the flag.

HAWAII

NIUE

The first Union Jack flag did not include the Irish cross of St. Patrick; it was added in 1801 upon the union of the kingdoms of Ireland and Great Britain.

Ireland returned to their independence in 1922, adopting a distinctly republican tricolor. The cross of St. Patrick, however, was kept to represent the part of Ireland that remained under British rule.

The British flag is also one of the most commonly seen elements among other flags of the world, whether national or regional flags.

TUVALU

ONTARIO

SAINT HELENA

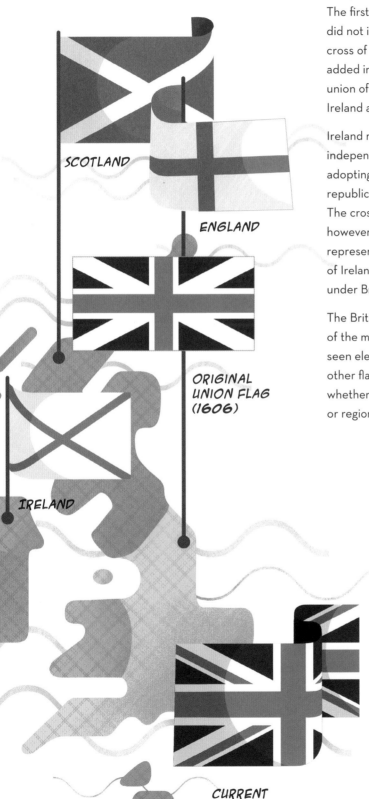

SCOTLAND

ENGLAND

ORIGINAL UNION FLAG (1606)

IRELAND

CURRENT UNION FLAG (1801)

You can find it in the flag of Oceania, in the cantons of the flags of Australia, New Zealand, Tuvalu and Fiji, in the flags of the regional states of Niue and Hawaii, in those of British Columbia and Ontario in Canada. Many remaining dependent territories still use the the Blue Ensign (which features the Union Jack as its canton). They are scattered throughout the world, whether they be islands swept by Antarctic winds, volcanoes in the middle of the ocean ruled by exiled emperors or small tropical paradises.

THE NETHERLANDS

The flag of the Netherlands is a horizontal tricolor consisting of red, white, and blue. Originally, it used orange instead of red. Tradition claims that the use of orange was in reference to William I of Orange, known as William the Silent, who led the Netherlands in a revolt against Spanish rule. This flag featuring orange, called the Prince's Flag, or Prinsenvlag, was also used by the so-called "gypsies of the sea"—a group of nobles who fought against Spanish rule.

By the 17th century, however, red began to take over as the prevailing color. It seems that the pigments used to dye the flag orange were unstable, and tended to darken over time. The orange and red versions alternated three times, from the end of the 16th century until 1816, the year in which the red version was finally decided upon. Orange, however, has remained the color with which the people of the Netherlands most identify themselves—from sports events to official parades, the Dutch streets are irrevocably tinged with orange.

CITY OF NEW YORK

The Dutch flag has a huge host of flags that followed: the most famous of these is the flag of Russia, which was directly inspired by the tricolor flag of the Netherlands. The Russian flag was then used as a model for many Slavic nations in Europe, including Serbia, Slovenia and the Czech Republic, so that the combination of red, white, and blue have now come to be called the Pan-Slavic colors.

REPUBLIC OF TRANSVAAL

Other flags that originate from the flag of the Netherlands can be found on the American continent: the flags of the cities of New York and Albany are descended from the Prince's Flag, evidenced by the color orange and the fact that both cities had Dutch origins.

There were also the flags of the Boer Republics in South Africa, such as Transvaal, the Orange Free State, and the Republic of Natalia.

ORANGE FREE STATE

REPUBLIC OF NATALIA

SCANDINAVIA

It has been said that those who share a flag also share points of view and opinions. The Scandinavian countries of Norway, Sweden, Finland and Denmark share much more. They are joined by their history, their culture and their languages. Their flags reflect this affinity and even though they are not exactly the same, they share a common base—the Scandinavian or Nordic Cross.

The initial success of this pattern began when Denmark adopted it in the thirteenth century. Legend has it that the characteristic design of the flag, a white cross on a red background, was not the creation of man but rather fell directly from the sky during a battle. As often happens in flag symbolism, the red background recalls a violent occasion.

DENMARK

Sweden was the second country to adopt the design but changed the colors to a blue field and a yellow cross, colors which were inspired by the background and the three gold crowns on the coat of arms of the Swedish King Magnus II who lived in the country's very distant past.

FINLAND

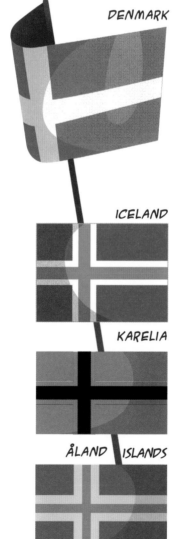

Norway also used the Danish design in its current flag, adopted only in 1821, but added a dark blue cross inside of the white one.

ICELAND

Finland joined the family in 1917 when it officially adopted its own version of the Scandinavian cross after a competition was held.

The design also encountered great success outside of Scandinavia. In 1918, Iceland was the last country to adopt a version with a Nordic Cross. But its flag's colors are inverted with respect to the Norwegian flag—it has a red cross fimbriated in white on a blue field.

KARELIA

SWEDEN

There are many regions, cities and administrative divisions that use a Scandinavian Cross, sometimes in opposition to the official flag—the Faroe Islands that are found between Iceland and Norway, the Åland Islands off the coast of Finland and Karelia in Russia.

ÅLAND ISLANDS

FAROE ISLANDS

GERMANY

Many nations of the world have their favorite color combinations, which have been used since ancient times with origins lost in legend. Germany, however, is a nation with a tradition of not just one, but two color combinations: black, red, and gold or black, white and red.

The flag that everyone is familiar with is one of the many tricolors from the revolutions during 1848 and it was made famous in a period known today as the Weimar Republic (1918-33). Times were difficult for Germany after their defeat in World War I but this period saw the flourish of art, architecture and culture in general.

The origins of the colors are unclear, but they seem to be a reference to the imperial banner of the Holy Roman Empire that has a black eagle with a red beak on a gold background.

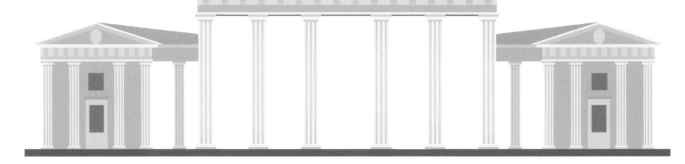

The German flag as we know it today has been used in three periods: between 1848 and 1852, between 1919 and 1933, and finally, from 1949 until today.

Another traditional color combination challenged the dominance of the colors of today's German flag: the combination of the colors of Prussia, black and white, with the colors of the Hanseatic League, red and white.

These colors have also been chosen many times, alternating with today's colors. Bismarck, for example, preferred them by far—he considered today's combination to be too revolutionary and too aggressive.

On July 20, 1944, both color combinations came into play. The Nazi party chose the black, white and red combination and replaced the national flag with their own symbol. Clearly, the Nazis did not respect the colors that recalled the Weimar Republic or its ideals of democracy and freedom of speech.

The German Resistance movement that tried to overthrow the Nazi regime, on the other hand, adopted the combination of gold, black, and red.

In 1949, Germany decided to use this gold, black and red combination, but with a classic tricolor design, to symbolize the democratic ideals that would inspire the country from that point forward.

CZECH REPUBLIC

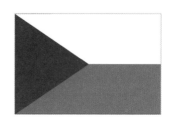

The flag of Czech, or the Czech Republic, is made up of two white and red horizontal bands, and one blue triangle to the left on the side of the hoist.

This is also the flag used by Czechoslovakia, when Czech and Slovakia were united. In 1993, the two countries split peacefully, and Czech kept the flag of Czechoslovakia, despite the protests of Slovakia.

Originally, the flag was simply white and red, the traditional colors of Bohemia, which came from an age-old coat of arms that showed a silver lion on a red background.

The design, however, was too similar to the flag of Poland, and differed only in terms of proportion. It was in 1920, after a competition to redesign the flag was won by Jaroslav Kursa, an archivist of the Czechoslovakian Interior Ministry, that the blue triangle was added. The addition made the flag more easily distinguishable and was aesthetically pleasing. It also associated the flag with others with that also used this combination of red, white, and blue—the Pan-Slavic colors.

Although there are no official meanings to these colors, they are traditionally associated with certain qualities and virtues. The red stands for courage and strength, the white for peace and honesty and the blue for vigilance, loyalty and justice.

SLOVAKIA

The history of Slovakia's flag is fairly brief. In 1993, after the country of Czechoslovakia was divided into two independent nations – the Czech Republic and Slovakia – Slovakia needed a flag.

The design for the center of the flag was entrusted to Ladislav Cisárik and Ladislav Vrtel, two heraldists, experts in vexillology and insignias. Based on drawings from the 14th century, they created a new symbol, a coat of arms, in which a double white cross stands on three blue hills on a red background.

The design embodies both the culture and the territory of the country: the cross is the symbol of Orthodox Christianity, one of the most characteristic elements of Slovak society and the three hills represent Slovakia's three mountains.

These two elements are also present on the flag of Slovenia whose coat of arms includes three mountains and on Hungary's flag that has the same Orthodox cross. The strong ties of these neighboring countries are also evident in the colors of their flags which are typical of the region: red, blue and white – to symbolize the unity and brotherhood of all Slavic populations.

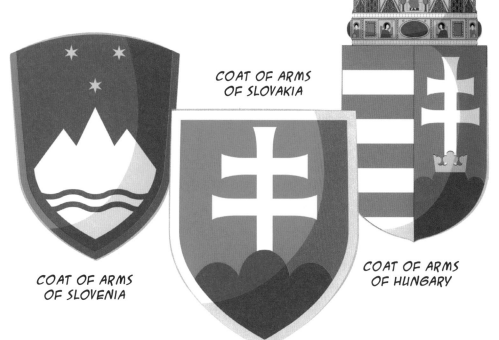

COAT OF ARMS
OF SLOVAKIA

COAT OF ARMS
OF SLOVENIA

COAT OF ARMS
OF HUNGARY

POLAND

The flag of Poland is an example of a flag that takes its colors from its coat of arms; its colors of red and white are the same ones used in the coat of arms of both Poland and Lithuania. This is because, between 1569 and 1795, these two countries were united in the Polish-Lithuanian Commonwealth—one of the biggest, most populous and most multi-ethnic nations of the time.

The Grand Duchy of Lithuania and the King of Poland had already formed a personal union at the end of the 14th century. For those who might not know, a personal union is when two different countries share the same sovereign, by virtue of marriage between two dynasties of rulers.

Therefore, there are two coats of arms—from which come the colors of the Polish flag—even though they both share the same colors. The Polish coat of arms features an eagle, while the Lithuanian coat of arms, called the Pahonia, features a brave knight riding a horse.

Legend has it that the ancient founder of Poland, by the name of Lech, saw an eagle in its nest framed by the last rays of sunset, with the pure white bird illuminated in such a way that its wings looked like they were golden. As to Lithuania, a medieval tale claims that the coat of arms with the knight on horseback was designed by Grand Duke Vytenis of Lithuania, but it seems more likely that the design was, in fact, already in use by then. The same coat of arms was later used in Belarus as well, which, at the time, was part of the Polish-Lithuanian Commonwealth.

Going back to the Polish eagle, it is a symbol that is well-loved and deeply felt by the Polish people—so much so that it has always appeared on revolutionary flags, whenever the country has needed to defend itself against the numerous invasions it has had to face over the centuries.

Today, like in the past, you can find the symbol on everything from coins to representative buildings, as well as—of course—other national emblems.

SHIELD OF LITHUANIA

SHIELD OF POLAND

HUNGARY

The flag of Hungary was born in the throes of revolution during 1848, the year in which all of Europe was affected by several anti-systemic movements and pro-republican uprisings. Like all revolutionary flags, it was inspired by the one of France—but, in order to avoid any confusion with the many tricolors that were in fashion during a time rife with revolution, the Hungarians wisely decided to place the bands horizontally rather than vertically.

The colors used have ancient origins, and according to tradition they symbolize strength with red, fidelity (or loyalty) with white and hope with green.

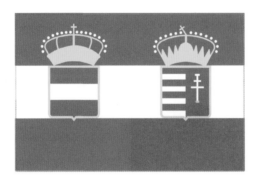

After the so-called "compromise" of 1867 signed with Austria, Hungary went from being a mere subject of the Austrian Empire to being considered its equal. Thus, the Austro-Hungarian Empire was born, and with it, an interesting flag created by combining the features of the Austrian and Hungarian flags.

Following World War I, Austria and Hungary split up and, at the end of World War II, Hungary became a satellite state of the Soviet Union.

During this period, the flag had a typically socialist coat of arms at its center.

In 1956, during the anti-Soviet uprising, this socialist and therefore hated emblem was systematically "cut out" from the middle flag, bringing the Hungarian flag back to its original design. It was a cry to the rest of the world about the struggle that the Hungarians faced and would have to overcome.

This is the story of how a flag with a missing emblem became a symbol of struggle and resistance.

RUSSIA

The flag of Russia was born out of the will of the Tsar Peter the Great. In 1693, the Tsar visited the city of Arkhangelsk to observe the construction of naval ships from Europe, and ordered a warship to be built by a Dutchman.

When the ship arrived, it was decorated with Dutch colors, and it was at that moment that the Tsar decided to rearrange them to create his own banner modeled after it.

The Dutch colors came to be associated with Russian and Pan-Slavic colors and became a model for dozens of flags for Slavic countries, such as Serbia, Slovakia and Croatia.

Despite practically uninterrupted use and great popularity, the flag only became the official national flag at the end of the 19th century—in 1883 to be exact.

Between 1858 and 1917, a competing flag appeared, with colors drawn from the colors of the imperial coat of arms, but it was eventually surpassed in popularity by the classic white-blue-red combination.

With the Russian Revolution following on the heels of World War I, the so-called red flags were introduced. They usually consisted of completely red fields, with socialist symbols like a hammer and sickle, or else Cyrillic writing or markings.

In 1922, Russia joined a federation of states known as the USSR, or Union of the Soviet Socialist Republics. The USSR flag followed the pattern of red flags and became the model for those of the republics that formed the Union.

Russia, now called the Russian Socialist Federal Republic of Russia (RSFSR), went from having a simple Cyrillic inscription reading "RSFSR" to a more elaborate design, consisting of the URSS flag with the addition of a vertical blue band.

Since 1991, with the dissolution of the USSR, Russia and other republics have returned to independence and after almost eighty years, have gone back to using the old symbols and flags that almost ended in oblivion. Russia, for its part, restored its beloved tricolor flag.

РСФСР

RUSSIAN RSFSR
(FROM 1954)

RUSSIAN RSFSR
(OLD)

SOVIET UNION

1858-1914

1923-1991

1925-1954

1954-1991

AFRICA

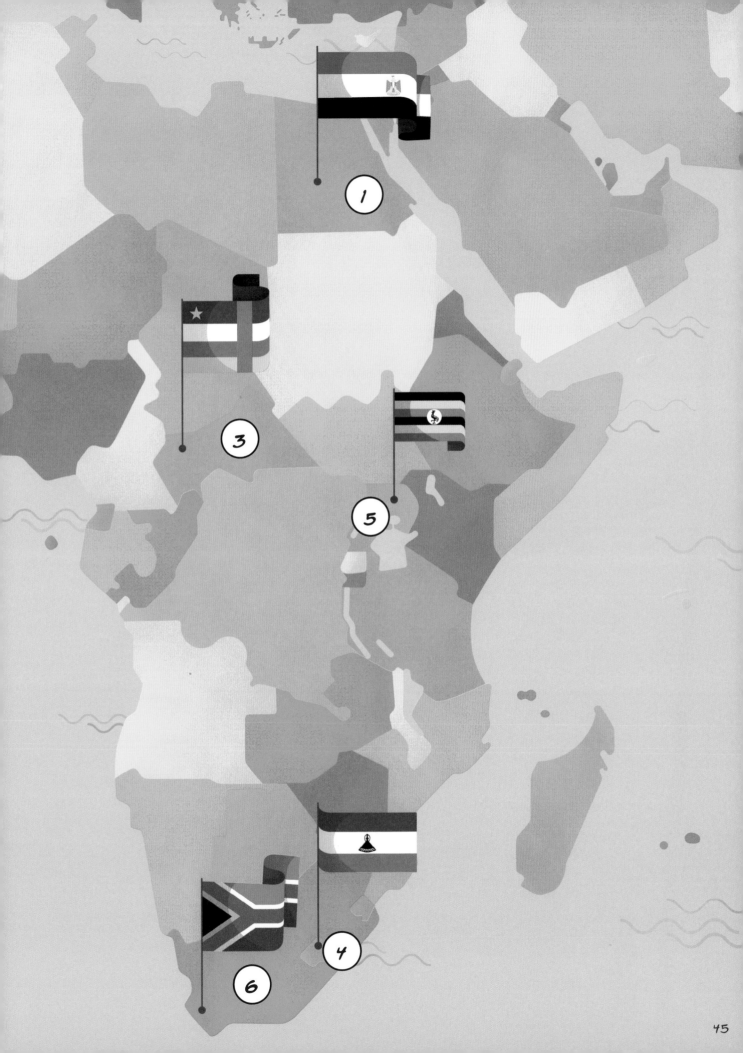

EGYPT

The Egyptian flag is a tricolor with the red, black and white stripes of the Arab Liberation flag. It dates back to time of the Egyptian Revolution in 1952.

The colors symbolize the various periods of the nation's history. Red represents the period before the revolution and the fight against the British Empire.

White is the symbol of the revolution that ended the monarchy in 1952 and black represents the future of the nation after the unseating of the monarchy and the end of British influence.

In the middle there is the eagle of Saladin, the first sultan of Syria and Egypt and the leader who fought against the crusades.

1867-1882

1844-1867

1882-1914

1914-1922

1922-1952

But Egypt's flag during the period of the monarchy was quite different. It had a symbol which was commonly used in Islamic culture: the star and crescent.

Green symbolized faith but also the fertility of the Nile and was in net contrast to the red of the Ottoman Empire.

This flag was substituted by one similar to today's during the brief existence of the UAR (United Arab Republic), in which for a short but intense period of time Syria and Egypt were politically united.

LIBERIA

The Liberian flag is made up of eleven red and white stripes and a blue canton with a white star at its center.

Its resemblance to the American flag, the first flag model to have stars and stripes, is readily evident.

This similarity is not a coincidence, in fact it was eagerly desired. Even though Liberia is an African state, its origins lie in the American continent.

In fact, Liberia was "created" by the American Colonization Society, a movement convinced that the freed African American slaves should return to their homeland.

The movement was made up of some very different factions. On one hand there were people who were sincerely convinced that this was the right solution for the freed slaves who they believed would be subject to discrimination and limitations even as free men. On the other hand there were openly racist people who believed that African Americans and whites were innately incompatible.

In any event, a colony was founded in Africa which later became the country named Liberia in honor of its population's newfound freedom.

The significance of the flag is clear. The settlers wanted to create a new country where they could pursue the American dream. The single star represents Liberia itself, the only country of its kind to have been founded in Africa at a time when European powers domineered on a continent almost completely colonized by foreigners.

REPUBLIC OF CENTRAL AFRICA

The flag of the Republic of Central Africa consists of four horizontal stripes: blue, white, green and yellow with a vertical red band in the middle. The star on the top near the hoist is a symbol of progress and prosperity.

This design combines the colors of France with the Pan-African colors in acknowledgement of both its past as a French colony and the future within the African community that it was building in those years.

The four stripes also represent the four territories that formed the French colony in equatorial Africa: Ubangi-Shari, Chad, Gabon and Congo, all of which are now part of other states.

The flag was adopted in 1960 which was known as "The Year of Africa" because it was the year in which the Central African Republic and many other countries obtained their independence.

FRENCH EQUATORIAL AFRICA

PROPOSAL OF BOKASSA

In 1976 a new flag was proposed by the President Jean Bedel Bokassa. The flag had a green background, a white and yellow canton and an Islamic crescent.

It was in that period that Bokassa had become close to Muammar Gaddafi, President of Libya, and converted to the Islamic religion. The predominant green color of the flag was surely tied to the Muslim religion and was a nod to the Libyan flag which is also completely green.

His plan for a new flag was probably an attempt to please his new ally but it was soon abandoned.

LESOTHO

The flag of Lesotho is a horizontal tricolor of green, white and blue. In the middle, it has an image of a mokorotlo, a cone-shaped hat used by the Sotho people who live in South Africa and Lesotho.

Folk history attributes the peculiar appearance of the hat to the shape of Qiloane, a mountain in Lesotho.

The colors represent the country's motto *Khotso Pula Nala*, which means "Peace, Rain and Abundance", concepts that correspond to the colors white, blue and green.

Lesotho substituted its previous flag in 2006 to eliminate symbols of war and to celebrate forty years of independence.

The old flag used Lesotho's traditional colors in diagonal stripes but it also had weapons and a golden shield.

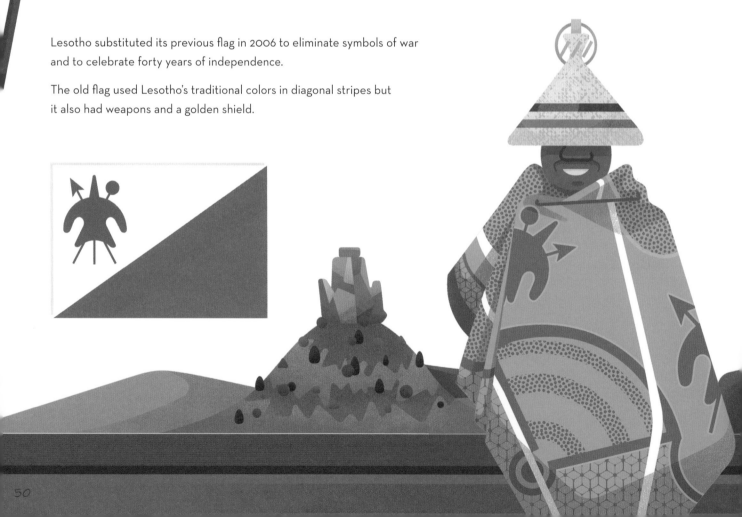

UGANDA

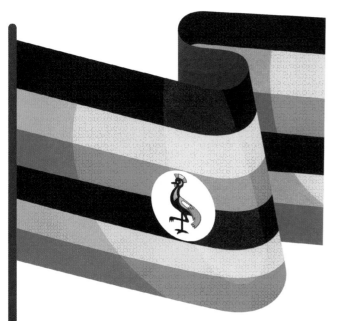

The flag of Uganda was adopted in 1962. It has six stripes in three colors: black, yellow and red which respectively represent Africa, the sun and brotherhood. At the center there is an emblem which depicts a crowned crane.

Like the countries of Kiribati and Barbados, Uganda incorporated elements of the old colonial flag into its new flag, something that was common in Britain's ex-colonies. The crowned crane on the old flag was depicted in a natural state while the crane on the new one is more stylized.

The emblem was also used on the first Ugandan flag, which was very short-lived. In fact, it was substituted by the present version for mostly political reasons. The colors green, yellow and blue were the colors of the Democratic Party of Uganda which was defeated in that year. The flag was designed by Grace Ibingira who was the Minister of Justice at the time.

SOUTH AFRICA

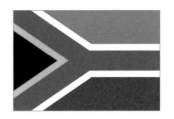

The flag of the Republic of South Africa has a truly particular design. It was created by the heraldist and vexillologist Fredrick Brownell.

Its six colors make the South African flag one of the most colorful in the world.

It is also rich in significance: the black, the yellow and the green are reminiscent of the colors of the African National Congress and represent the black population.

The red, white and blue symbolize both the Dutch tricolor and the flag of the United Kingdom and represent the white population including the English and Afrikaners. The Y shape symbolizes two branches that meet to form one, perfectly representing two populations united for a better future.

This flag was created in 1994 after the release of Nelson Mandela from prison. Mandela was the leader of the anti-apartheid movement and South Africa's first black president. He won the Nobel Peace Prize together with the Klerk, his Afrikaner counterpart, for ending the regime of oppression and the segregation of the black population.

AFRICAN NATIONAL CONGRESS

$+$

UNITED KINGDOM

$+$

THE NETHERLANDS

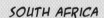

SOUTH AFRICA

The previous flag was seen as a symbol of this oppression and of the country's dark past.

The old flag was a Dutch-born Prinsenvlag with three smaller flags in the middle: the flags of the United Kingdom, of the Orange Free State and of the South African Republic, often referred to as Transvaal. The flags were placed there in an attempt to satisfy all of the national groups in the country. It was a mess.

The intent was to recognize both the Dutch speaking Afrikaner and the English communities but the result was confusing to say the least. The new flag does a clearly better job at uniting all of the colors, including those representing Africa, in a unique and original design.

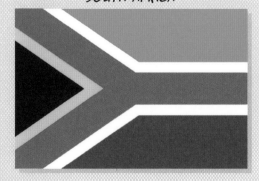

ASIA

TURKEY

The Ottoman Empire began using the Turkish flag as we know it today around 1793, during the reign of Selim III, but apparently it had already been in use for thirty years.

Legend attributes its origin to a rather surreal dream that the founder of the Ottoman Empire, none other than Osman I, had. He dreamed that a star and a waxing moon rose out of his chest and exploded. Another legend speaks of the battles of the European Empire, more precisely in Kosovo, where the Sultan Murad saw a star and a moon reflected in a pool of blood.

But the history of the star and crescent is much more ancient. They were used in antiquity in the Middle East. Constantinople, Turkey's capital which later became Istanbul, was once known as Byzantium and had the Greek goddess Artemis as its protector; her symbol was a waxing moon.

So the star, thought to be Venus, was one of the brightest and most important celestial bodies after the Moon and the Sun and was therefore fundamental to the ancient observers of the sky.

Even before the current flag, red was a prevalent color in the flags used by the Ottomans, both on ships and on land. There was a time when the flag was green, the color of Islam. It lasted for sixty years until the adoption of the famous crescent moon. For a long time the morning star had eight points, then it was redesigned with five points to give it a more European flavor.

MERCANTILE FLAG FOR THE MUSLIM REGIONS

The Ottomans created mercantile flags for their empire: a red flag with a green band for the Muslim regions and a red flag with a blue band for the Christian regions, such as Greece.

When Turkey transitioned from an Empire to a Republic, its flag remained the same. The star and crescent became a symbol of the Islamic religion and of the unification of its followers. The vastness of the Ottoman State accounts for the use of the same symbol on the flag of many other Asian and African countries.

MERCANTILE FLAG FOR THE CHRISTIAN REGIONS

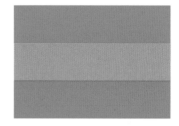

UNITED ARAB EMIRATES

The flag of the United Arab Emirates is a good example of the use of Pan-Arabic colors: green, white and black. In 1971, Abdullah Mohammed Al Maainah who is now the ambassador to Chile, won a competition to design the flag at the age of nineteen.

But the future ambassador did not know that his design had been selected. The designs of the six finalists were published in black and white in the newspapers, so Al Maainah had no way of knowing whether his had been chosen until he ran to the Royal Palace on the day of the inauguration.

There was no wind that day so the boy had to wait for a gentle breeze to finally see his flag! His creation has been with him ever since, especially now with his many diplomatic trips around the world.

Before becoming the federation that we know today, individual emirates were divided entities. It was the Emirates of Dubai and Abu Dhabi who invited the other emirates to form a union. Bahrein and Qatar declined the offer, while Ajman, Fujairah, Ras al-Khaimah, Sharjah and Umm al-Quwain agreed.

All of the flags of the emirates have the red and white colors in common. The colors originate in the red cloth that had been used since the 18th century, when the area was known as the Pirate Coast. In 1820 after the non-aggression treaty with the British was signed, a white border was added to the flag and all future flags would stem from this design.

RAS AL-KHAIMAH AND SHARJAH

ABU DHABI

UMM AL-QAIWAIN

FUJAIRAH UNTIL 1972

الفجيرة

AJMAN AND DUBAI

ISRAEL

The Israeli flag finds its origins in the United States in 1891, almost sixty years before the state of Israel was founded in 1948. In fact, it was flown by the prisoners freed from Buchenwald in 1945.

The flag was presented by a certain Mr. Askowith and his son at the inauguration of a Jewish school in Boston. It was very similar to today's flag with exception of the word "Maccabee" written on it.

The writing was later removed, just as the good rules of flag design require.

A few years later, the flag was adopted by the Zionist movement, a political religious movement whose purpose was the creation of a Jewish state in Palestine.

Another very similar version was prepared for the Zionist Congress of Basel in 1898; it had blue bands that covered the flag to the edges.

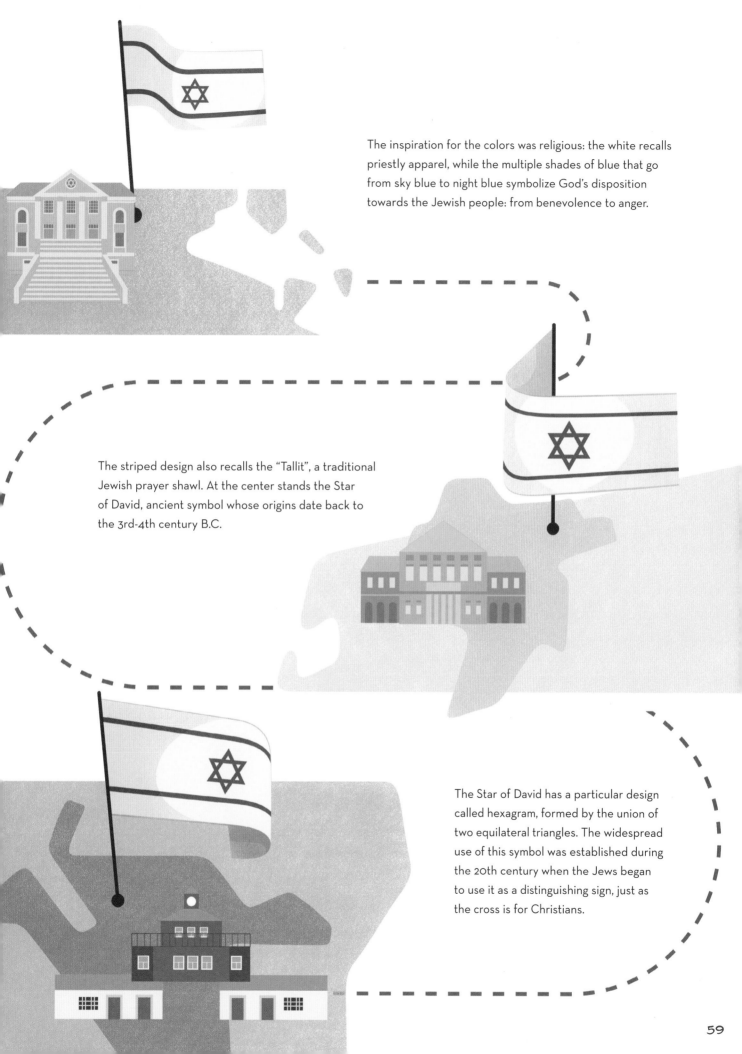

The inspiration for the colors was religious: the white recalls priestly apparel, while the multiple shades of blue that go from sky blue to night blue symbolize God's disposition towards the Jewish people: from benevolence to anger.

The striped design also recalls the "Tallit", a traditional Jewish prayer shawl. At the center stands the Star of David, ancient symbol whose origins date back to the 3rd-4th century B.C.

The Star of David has a particular design called hexagram, formed by the union of two equilateral triangles. The widespread use of this symbol was established during the 20th century when the Jews began to use it as a distinguishing sign, just as the cross is for Christians.

INDIA

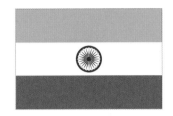

Indian citizens love their flag. It was adopted in 1947 when India gained its independence from Britain. Its colors are those of the Indian National Congress, the party guided by key figures such as Mahatma Gandhi and Jawaharlal Nehru that became one of the main champions of India's independence.

India's tricolor is known as Tiranga. Each of its colors has a different meaning: the particular shade of orange (called "saffron") symbolizes courage and sacrifice, the white is for purity, and the green represents faith and the cavalry.

Another widespread interpretation states that the saffron and green represent the two major religions of the country: Hinduism and Islamism.

The central symbol is a chakra called *Dharmachakra*, or the "Wheel of Law". It was inspired by the one carved on the famous capital of the Lions of the ancient sovereign Ashoka, who used the symbol for his royal edicts.

In earlier versions, the shape of the symbol was similar but its meaning was completely different.

The wheel was a spinning wheel suggested by Gandhi as a symbol of the autonomy and self-sufficiency of the Indian people. The message was clear: those who can weave their own clothes are self-sufficient.

So it was that the flag proposed by Gandhi and designed by Pingali Venkayya became the flag of the party, then the flag of independence and finally of the nation.

SOUTH KOREA

The Koreans did not feel the necessity for a national flag until their relations with other nations intensified during the 19th century. At diplomatic meetings, other nations displayed their own flags and even though the Korean Emperor initially gave little importance to the issue, he eventually decided to create a flag that he could proudly exhibit at these meetings. The central circle and the proportions of the original flag were slightly different than those of today's flag but the general appearance has remained the same.

Despite their initial disinterest in flags, the Koreans did a splendid job. The final result, was one of the most meaningful and beautiful flags ever to be made.

The word that best describes this flag is balance. In fact, the elements of the flag are no more than a series of individual parts which, when combined, represent the world around us. The central circle is divided into two sections following the philosophical concept of Yin and Yang, which requires that opposite forces such as light and shadow, positive and negative, be in balance and dependent on one another.

The four symbols surrounding the circle are called trigrams (in Korean *Gwae* or *Kwae*), because they consist of three overlapping bars. The four trigrams may be simple in appearance but they have a myriad of meanings; so many in fact, that it would be impossible to describe them all!

☰ (*Geon*) represents the Heaven, the spring, humanity and the father figure. ☵ (*Gam*) symbolizes the Moon, winter, intelligence and the son figure. ☷ (*Gon*) summarises the Earth, summer, courtesy and the mother figure. ☲ (*Ri*), the last trigram, is associated with the Sun, autumn, justice and the daughter figure.

As you may have guessed, the elements in the trigrams represent the four seasons, four celestial bodies, four virtues, a small family and the four cardinal points as well.

By doing so, Korea has successfully incorporated an extraordinary amount of symbols and meanings into a simple, concise design.

PEOPLE'S REPUBLIC OF CHINA

When a competition was held to choose China's flag, a huge number of designs were proposed, all of which had one element in common: the color red. In fact, the use of this color was one of the specific requirements stated in the call for proposals.

The winning proposal was designed by Zheng Liansong. This winning design is an example of the family of red flags that are similar to the flag of the ex-Soviet Union. The red of the Chinese flag symbolizes revolutionary and socialist ideals but it also represents the Han ethnicity which is the largest in the country.

There are five stars in the canton, the flag's place of honor. One is larger than the others and represents the Chinese Communist Party.

The original intent of the designer was that the other four stars were to represent the four social classes of the nation: the workers, the farmers, the middle class and the upper class as they were described by Mao Zedong in a famous speech. Even Mao himself proposed a design.

The stars are positioned in a semi-circle to convey the idea of a population united regardless of social position.

MAO ZEDONG'S PROPOSAL

Before becoming the People's Republic of China, from 1912 to 1928, the country had an interesting flag known as the "Five Races Under One Union".

The colors of the flag represented the five major ethnic groups present in China: red for the Han, yellow for the Manchurians, blue for the Mongolians, white for the Hui and black for the Tibetans.

A short-lived second version utilized the same colors but in the shape of a saltire or a St. Andrew's Cross.

Another flag was proposed by the Chinese Nationalist Party or the Kuomintang and was used from the 1930's until the foundation of the People's Republic in 1949.

This has been the flag used in Taiwan, or the Republic of China, since the time of the civil war, when the Kuomintang retreated to the island and founded the Republic of China, taking the flag with them.

TAIWAN

JAPAN

The flag of Japan is one that is distinct, immediately recognizable and famous throughout the world. There is no need to be an expert to recognize this flag even if it was not officially adopted until 1999. We will come back to the flag's history after we talk about its design and symbolism.

The design is composed of a red circle on a white background and certainly respects the first rule of good flag design—simplicity.

The flag's meaning is quite simple too—it is the name of the country. The red circle represents the "Rising Sun."

The Japanese call Japan *Nihon* or *Nippon*. The *kanji* that form the word Japan are 日本, and literally mean "Birth of the Sun". They can be pronounced Ni (日) and Hon (本).

The name "Japan" in English and French is a mispronunciation derived from the Chinese pronunciation of the two symbols. The name Nippon, as opposed to Nihon, is used in formal occasions, such as ceremonies or sporting events.

Japan has called itself the Land of the Rising Sun for a long time. In 607, in a letter written to China, the Sovereign's rather pompous letter head read "Emperor of the Rising Sun".

HIROSHIMA

FUKUOKA

SAITAMA

OKINAWA

The association with the rising sun stems from Japan's geographical position. It is the last Asian land before the Pacific Ocean and so the land everyone looks towards to see the rising sun. Some say the name originated in China and refers to Japan's eastern position relative to that country.

The Japanese have a tormented opinion of their own flag and in fact it took until 1999 to decree its official adoption.

Some Japanese fear that the flag could be associated with the country's militaristic and dictatorial past but others have a different opinion. The flag was already in use after the World War II, when Japan was given permission to use it once again, so the law did nothing more than confirm what was already in common use.

The flags of the Japanese prefectures are an example of good flag design. Some recall the Japanese flag in their choice of color and design and they all use the model of one symbol on a neutral background.

OCEANIA

4

3

2

AUSTRALIA

The Australian flag is a Blue Ensign of British origin with a Southern Cross and a Commonwealth Star.

The Blue Ensign is a blue flag with the flag of the United Kingdom in the canton, the Southern Cross is a popular symbol among the countries of the Southern Hemisphere, and the Commonwealth Star represents Australia itself with its seven points symbolizing the nation's states and territories and the capital district.

The flag was adopted in 1903 when the Commonwealth Star still had its original six points.

The opinions about the flag are rather controversial. Many citizens love their flag and strongly identify with it while others believe it to be too heavily tied to the country's colonial past and are moving to create a new one. They argue that the flag does not represent a clearly Australian identity and they also think that it is too similar to New Zealand's flag.

After all, the current flag strongly resembles the National Colonial Flag for Australia and the subsequent Australian Federation Flag which were designed to bolster an Australian national identity despite the continuing strong ties to the United Kingdom.

The design for the flag of Australia is always a hot topic for debate and the number of new proposals grows every year. It is literally impossible to list them all but here is a short presentation of the most loved alternatives.

The flag designed by Brett Moxey, the "Southern Horizon", combines the beloved symbols of the Southern Cross and the Commonwealth Star with Australia's traditional colors: green and gold, the colors worn by athletes at national sporting events. The Southern Horizon appears to be the most popular alternative to the current flag.

Another interesting flag design is known as the "Golden Wattle" or "Golden Acacia", a tree which can be found all over Australia. The designer used elements that are reminiscent of the acacia flower to suggest the Commonwealth Star without actually drawing it.

The flag designed by Tone Moore is one of the many that propose the image of the kangaroo as a unifying element for the communities of British descent and Aboriginal Australians.

Many maintain that the colors of the Aboriginal Australian flag (red, black and yellow) must be included in the final design of the new flag.

NEW ZEALAND

The flag of New Zealand is modelled after the British Blue Ensign, the colonial flag widely used throughout the world at the time of the British Empire.

Today, flags based on the Blue Ensign model are used in three other Oceanian countries—Australia, Fiji and Tuvalu—as well as in the few remaining British Crown Dependencies. This flag became official in 1902.

Opposite the canton with the British flag are four red stars with white fimbriation that make up the constellation of the Southern Cross, a common symbol for the states and territories of the Southern Hemisphere.

The first New Zealand flag was not the Blue Ensign; it was agreed upon when independence from the United Tribes of New Zealand was declared in 1835. The agreement was signed by Maori chiefs and by British colonial authorities.

The flag, designed by the missionary Henry Williams, included clearly English elements and was selected by the Maori chiefs for its abundance of red, a color of particular importance for them, and for the Christian Cross. New Zealand's ships finally had an international symbol.

In around 1860, with the consolidation of the power of the United Kingdom, the Blue Ensign was adopted. The first version simply had the letters "NZ", while the second had the four stars of the Southern Cross in a diamond shape, not as they are today.

In 2015 and 2016, after decades of debates and discussions, a referendum was held to decide upon the changes in New Zealand's flag.

As in Australia and Fiji, there are groups that push for the adoption of a new symbol, mainly for three reasons: the current flag is too similar to that of Australia and creates confusion between two nations of such close proximity; the flag is in effect a colonial symbol and so, many believe, unsuitable for an independent nation, and finally, the current symbols only represent the population of British descent and neglect the Maori population.

Five proposals for a new flag were presented to the population. Three used the silver fern, a strongly felt symbol in New Zealand and two of these three also had the Southern Cross constellation. They use either the traditional colors of the New Zealand flag—red, white and blue—or another very popular color—black.

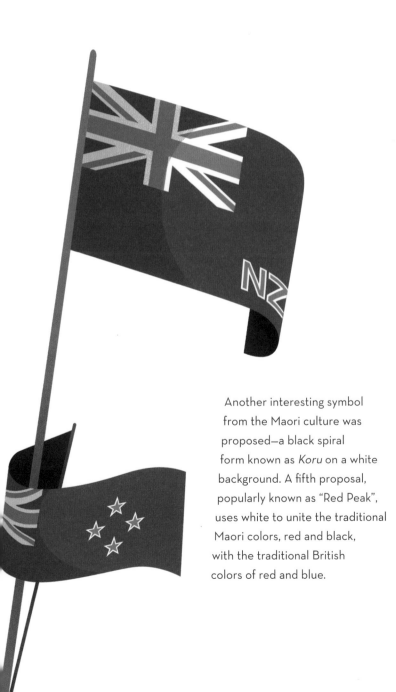

Another interesting symbol from the Maori culture was proposed—a black spiral form known as *Koru* on a white background. A fifth proposal, popularly known as "Red Peak", uses white to unite the traditional Maori colors, red and black, with the traditional British colors of red and blue.

VANUATU

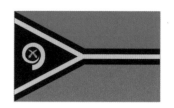

The flag of Vanuatu has two green and red stripes overlapped by a black triangle and a yellow, horizontal Y shape with black fimbriation. At the center of the triangle is a wild boar tusk encircling two fronds of namele, a local plant.

The flag took its colors from the flag of the independence party, the Vanua'aku Pati, and each one has a precise meaning: the green symbolizes the earth's richness, the red represents the blood shed by the people, the black symbolizes the population itself and the yellow symbolizes Christianity. The Y is representative of the shape of the Vanuatu island chain.

The curved wild boar's tusk symbolizes wealth and the islanders wear it as an ornament.

The plants represented have 39 leaves, the number of members in Vanuatu's parliament and are therefore a symbol of democracy.

The flag of Vanuatu was adopted in 1980 when the archipelago became independent from not one but two nations simultaneously: the United Kingdom and France. As a matter of fact, the islands once known as the New Hebrides were under the joint control of these two nations.

During the Pacific Games, when Vanuatu was still under the administration of the United Kingdom and France, its flag was a combination of smaller versions of both the French and the British flag: certainly not the best design choice. The archipelago has redeemed itself with the adoption of one of the most beautiful and distinctive flags of the Pacific.

KIRIBATI

The Republic of Kiribati is a nation made up of islands and atolls scattered over a surface twice the size of Alaska. Its flag is a perfect example of an armorial banner and of the recycling of old symbols in a new way.

An armorial banner, in fact, has the same image as a coat of arms, a crest or an emblem for example, that extends to the entire flag.

The country's previous flag was the British Blue Ensign with a classic Union Jack in the canton and a shield in the fly.

When independence was granted in 1979, a competition was held. The design that won was actually the old emblem with modified proportions.

The wavy white stripes symbolize the country's strong ties to the Pacific Ocean and the three main island groups: the Gilbert Islands, the Line Islands and the Phoenix Islands.

The golden bird is a frigatebird with very long wings and the ability to cover huge distances such as those that separate the archipelagos. The frigatebird symbolizes dominion over the seas and the sunset that generates the red background symbolizes the proximity of Kiribati to the equator.

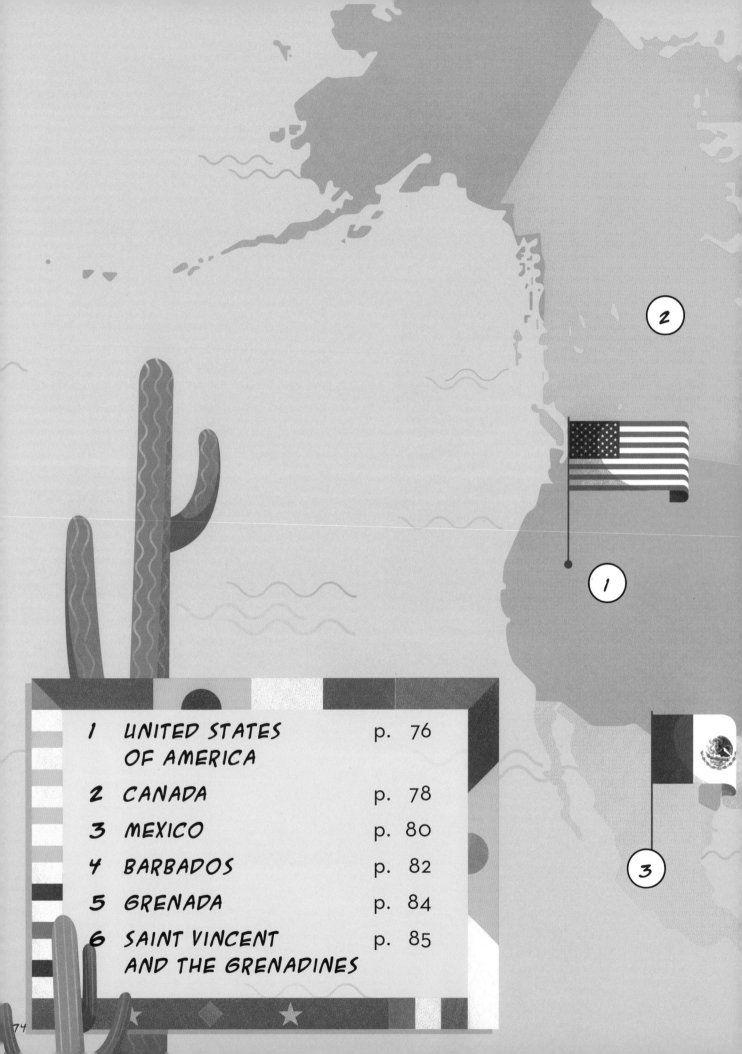

NORTH AND CENTRAL AMERICA

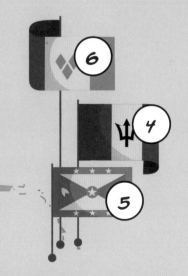

6

4

5

UNITED STATES OF AMERICA

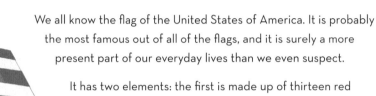

We all know the flag of the United States of America. It is probably the most famous out of all of the flags, and it is surely a more present part of our everyday lives than we even suspect.

It has two elements: the first is made up of thirteen red and white horizontal stripes, and the second is a blue canton with fifty white stars. The stripes represent the first thirteen British colonies that gained their independence from the British Crown on July 4, 1776, eventually becoming the first united states, while the fifty stars represent each of the states that make up the country today. However, the original meaning of the colors is still a mystery, though many meanings have been attributed to them.

This flag has several nicknames, and is commonly called "Stars and Stripes", "Old Glory" and "The Star-Spangled Banner". Even the blue rectangle with its stars has its own name: "The Union."

The name "Stars and Stripes" has become synonymous with America and this shows how important the flag is to Americans, who identify strongly with it.

The flag is one of the most famous and most well-known in the world, becoming a symbol of pop culture worldwide in addition to its home base. Though we might not realize it, we see it very often: in comic books with Superman and Captain America (who is practically outfitted with an American flag), to the movie theatre where it is almost omnipresent, to album covers, and even at times in fashion. It is often revised, modified, and at times even abused; these changes, however, make up part of the flag's history.

At the time the flag was adopted, there were only thirteen, not fifty states. To welcome the new states, added over the course of its two-hundred and fifty years of history, the U.S. government added new stars to the blue canton to reflect the changes in the union that the canton represented.

But how was this flag created? The United States of America was born out of a war—and, like in all wars, there was confusion about which symbols to adopt, at least at the beginning. The various flags carried by the military groups who fought for independence used many different symbols, from the moon to snakes. For example, the yellow flag featuring a rattlesnake was one of the most threatening flags, practically a message in and of itself on the battlefield against the British. The writing, in fact, announced, "DON'T TREAD ON ME"—that is, do not trample on me, or you will be hurt!

Alternatively, the second flag used was full of hope: together, the moon and the word "LIBERTY" represented a desire for a better, and freer, future.

When the United States of America finally became independent, it was time to have a flag of its own. The very first versions—probably in the hopes of remaining on good terms—showed the British flag in its canton, in place of the stars.

GRAND UNION (6 MONTHS)

HOPKINSON

Six months later, it was decided that there would be stars to represent the states, but no one knew exactly how the flag would be designed and arranged. The result was a number of flags with evident variations: some had stars arranged in a line, some in a circle and who knows in how many other ways.

It was Francis Hopkinson, author and composer, as well as New Jersey delegate, to design the first version (it is rumored that he received an initial payment in wine and only later in actual money). But popular legend asserts that it was Betsy Ross who sewed the first flag, directly from a drawing given to her by George Washington himself.

Even if the latter is a rather hasty explanation, it is nevertheless a much-loved legend. Certainly, it is much more captivating to think of a graceful lady sewing according to Washington's instructions, rather than a grumpy composer-poet, who argued over the right kind of payment for his efforts.

Slowly, as states have been added to the country, so have stars to the flag. The stripes, however, have never been changed, except for an attempt in 1795 to change the thirteen stripes to fifteen.

The last star to be added was Hawaii, the last state to join the union in 1959. Although fifty is, no doubt, a nice, round number, and easy to represent in a neat row of stars, what will happen to the flag if another state were to be added? This is not an entirely unlikely event, given that there are some territories, such as the capital district of Washington D.C., and the American territory of Puerto Rico, where there are movements whose goal it is to have the island be accepted and recognized as a new state. Thankfully, there are already many ways available in order to add an extra state—some that are more traditional, and some that are quite particular.

Even if the American flag slightly alters its appearance, it will always remain one of the most recognizable and irreplaceable symbols. Without it, art, cinema and culture certainly would not have been the same as we know them today.

"BETSY ROSS" VARIATION

OLD GLORY (48 STARS)

CANADA

The Canadian flag looks like a white stripe running down the center background, with a red maple leaf in the very middle.

When the flag was designed and made official in 1965, the maple leaf was already a symbol that the Canadians had used for some time, since the end of the 18th century.

But the choice of design for the flag was very controversial. The debate over the flag began thanks to Egypt, a country that is certainly not the first place to come to mind when thinking about the snow and ice associated with Canada.

In 1956, Israel attacked Egypt in what is known as the Sinai War, or the Suez Crisis. After the attack, France and the United Kingdom came together in attempt to overthrow the Egyptian presidency of Nasser and recapture strategic control of the Suez Canal.

During the war, Canada became involved as a peacekeeper, in the midst of a tense and highly complicated situation.

Egyptians complained that since the old flag of Canada looked too similar to the flag of the United Kingdom they were allied politically. This compromised the supposed neutrality of Canada.

Lester Pearson—who was the Minister of External Affairs after having won a Nobel Peace Prize for, in fact, managing the Egyptian crisis so well—took this issue to heart and promised to adopt a new symbol.

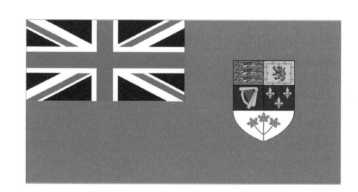

SUEZ CRISIS - 1956

If, for the English-speaking population of Canada, the old flag remained all in all quite popular, it was, for the French-speaking population based in Quebec, perhaps not the most welcome symbol. The question became more about whether or not to keep the British flag, called "Union Jack," in its canton rather than whether or not to adopt the already-beloved symbol of the maple leaf.

One of the most famous proposals was favored by Pearson himself —in fact, today, this design is still known as Pearson's Pennant.

In the design, there are three maple leaves, like in the old coat of arms, and the colors of the bands on the sides were blue instead of red.

In 1964, a special commission was set up to put an end to the bickering that had inflamed Parliament for months. The committee reviewed proposals by the thousands—in fact, more than three thousand designs, symbols, and ideas flooded their desks for weeks on end. A great number of these included the image of a maple leaf, while some others included the British Union Jack or the French fleur-de-lis.

In the end, the committee chose a design submitted by George Stanley, a Canadian historian, who held the firm view that the flag should not have any kind of symbols that might divide the country.

Despite its tumultuous origin, the Canadian flag is highly appreciated for its simple and impactful design, and, since 1996, Canada has even dedicated a national holiday to celebrating its flag.

MEXICO

The flag of Mexico is a green, white, and red tricolor, with an extremely elaborate national coat of arms at the center. The colors come from the national liberation army, called the Garantista, who fought against the Spanish during the Mexican War of Independence.

The flag used then was nicknamed the Army of the Three Guarantees, with the white, green and red symbolizing, in order, the religion, independence and unity of the Mexican people. Before adopting the current version, the independent movement used a multitude of symbols, many flags depicting, for example, religious symbols like the Virgin Mary.

The national coat of arms shows a Mexican eagle perched on a cactus, in the act of eating a rattlesnake. The image references an ancient Aztec legend regarding the foundation of Mexico City.

THREE GUARANTEES

The god Huitzilopochtli advised the Aztecs to search for an eagle like the one described, when choosing the location to found a new city. Supposedly, the Aztecs did, in fact, find an eagle rested atop a rock on an island, in the middle of a lake—just as it is represented in the coat of arms.

This symbol holds a long-established religious and cultural meaning. The flag, however, did not immediately bring all of these elements together in the same design—as you see it today—but rather, slowly added them.

The Mexican flag is very similar to the Italian flag, with slight exceptions: the inclusion of the coat of arms, the darker shade of green, and the proportions.

The flag of the Italian Navy displays the coat of arms of the maritime republics, in order to differentiate itself from the flag of the Mexican army, which, at one time, was free from any heraldry or coats of arms.

BARBADOS

Barbados is a lush Caribbean island and as such, its flag uses blue to symbolize the sea, and yellow to symbolize the sand on its beaches.

The trident, associated with Neptune and thus with the larger theme of the ocean, is also a strong symbol of freedom. The former Barbados flag was a Blue Ensign, like all of the British colonies, and the coat of arms showed a woman with a trident in hand.

The woman was none other than Britannia, or rather, the colonizing power that governed Barbados, and the trident of Neptune represented British dominance of the seas.

The man who designed the Barbados flag, an art teacher by the name of Grantley Prescod, decided to change the trident to a broken one in the middle of the flag, as a clear symbol of the end of colonial rule.

The three points of the trident represent the three democratic principles important to Prescod: government of the people, for the people, by the people.

Prescod's design was chosen out of thousands of other proposals in a competition. He had already prepared seven well-studied proposals but the design that was eventually chosen was actually made in a hurry on the morning of the competition.

GRENADA

The design of the flag of the island of Grenada is really something special: it is formed by four green and yellow triangles—reminiscent of a saltire, or a cross, similar to the one of Jamaica—and it has a red border with six stars inside it to represent the six parishes of the island.

The star encircled by a red disc in the middle represents the island of Carriacou, the largest of the Grenadine islands—which are made up of Grenada, Saint Vincent and the Grenadines.

To the left, next to the hoist, we find a stylized image of a nutmeg—an incredibly important product for the economy of the island, and one that recalls the previous name of Grenada, Spice Island. Red represents courage, yellow the sun, and green the nature.

The previous flag, which was used for seven years when Grenada became a state associated with the United Kingdom, also depicted a nutmeg, but one that was more natural and less stylized than the current version.

The previous colors alluded to the island's bountiful nature.

SAINT VINCENT AND THE GRENADINES

The flag of Saint Vincent and the Grenadines is a blue, yellow, and green tricolor, with an emblem formed by three diamonds at the very center.

The yellow band in the middle is twice as large as the others, and represents the golden beaches of this little group of Caribbean islands. In contrast, the blue recalls the sky and seas, while the green represents its lush natural landscape.

The emblem in the center is made up of diamonds, in assertion that these islands are the jewels of the Caribbean. In addition, these diamond shapes form the letter V, which stands for Vincent.

Prior to adopting this particular design, the flag of Saint Vincent and the Grenadines displayed another emblem that was much more detailed, but perhaps less suitable for a flag and rather, more suited to a coat of arms; it showed the leaf of a breadfruit plant, along with two female figures that represent peace and justice, dressed in Roman garments —an image clearly derived from the British colonial flag.

PAX ET JUSTITIA

SOUTH AMERICA

COLOMBIA

The flag of Colombia is a horizontal yellow, blue, and red tricolor. However, the three bands are not all the same size; the yellow stripe is twice as big as both the red and blue stripes. Tradition states that the color yellow represents gold from the South American continent, the blue its oceans, and the red the blood spilled in the battle for independence.

This flag is similar to the ones of Ecuador and Venezuela, so that together, the three flags create a little independent family of flags.

The reason for this resemblance is that these states became independent under the direction of Simon Bolivar. After the dismemberment of New Granada they were originally united under a single state called Gran Colombia.

Gran Colombia arose from the ashes of New Granada, which was one of the Viceroyalties of Spain in South America. At the beginning of the 19th century, the local population began to resist Spanish rule and call for independence from the Spanish Crown.

The Venezuelan general Francisco de Miranda designed their first flag, which later inspired the flag of Gran Colombia.

PANAMA

GRAN COLOMBIA

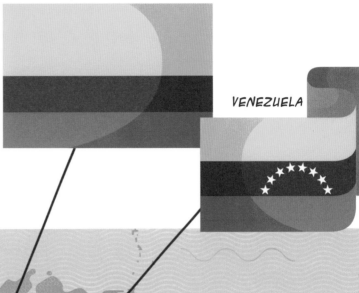

VENEZUELA

NEW GRANADA

ECUADOR

It seems that the idea of using primary colors for the flag stemmed from a conversation that Miranda had with the German writer Johann Wolfgang von Goethe, who explained the theory of primary colors: that, in painting, red, yellow and blue are the only colors you need to create any and all of the other colors. Miranda liked the idea of creating a nation whose few colors had the potential to create all others.

Goethe also affirmed that the first thing that a nation needed to do in order to establish itself was to decide upon a name and a flag.

Miranda also cited another source of inspiration—the frescos of the artist Lazzaro Tavarone, in the Palazzo Belimbau in Genoa, Italy, depicting Christopher Columbus upon his return from the Americas.

However, Gran Colombia failed and the countries that participated in the project have only their flags as mementoes of that brief period, with its ideals of rebellion and liberty.

GUYANA

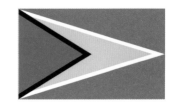

The Guyana flag has a very dynamic and impressive design thanks to the hand of Whitney Smith, a renowned vexillologist and researcher. Whitney coined the term "vexillology", namely the study of flags. He was also the first to publish a periodical dedicated to flags: "The Flag Bulletin".

Each of the colors has a symbolic meaning: the green stands for the agricultural richness and natural wealth, the yellow for the mining, the red for the dynamism of the nation, the white for the rivers and the black for the force of its people.

Smith participated in the competition that Guyana launched to decide upon a flag when it gained independence in 1966.

But his original design was different; it did not have the black and white fimbriation and according to some, the green and red stripes were inverted. It is thought to have been the College of Arms, the highest authority in the field of heraldry and flags, that suggested the changes. The truth is that the flag breaks one of the most sacred heraldic rules: never put the colors of two metals such as gold and silver, that is yellow and white, side by side.

As we have learned, you can break the design rules and still produce a beautiful flag and Guyana's golden arrow is a perfect example.

FROM 1875 TO 1906

FROM 1906 TO 1955

FROM 1955 TO 1966

CHILE

Its simplicity has made Chile's flag one of the best liked flags in South America. It has two horizontal stripes, one red and one white and a blue square canton which contains the five pointed star that gives the flag its name: "Estrella Solitaria".

The white stands for the snow of the Andes Mountain Range which runs the length of the country, the blue is for the sky and the red symbolizes the blood which was shed in the struggle for independence.

Tradition suggests that the choice of colors reflects the symbols used by the Mapuche in their insurrection against the Spanish.

The blue star in the canton is also linked to the Mapuche symbols. Their war insignia featured Venus, known as the morning star, depicted as a particular eight-pointed star on a blue diamond-shaped field bordered in red and yellow.

FROM 1812 TO 1814

FROM 1817 TO 1818

FROM OCTOBER 1817

BRAZIL

Besides being well loved and appreciated by its citizens, the Brazilian flag is one of the most widely recognized in the world. Today the flag and its colors represent Brazil's personality and you will always find it at center stage during World Cup soccer games in what became the legendary *torcida*, the festive and wild cheer of the Brazilian fans.

The flag has a yellow diamond on a green background with a blue circle in the center. There are 27 white stars inside the blue circle that represent each of the states in the Brazilian Federation. Originally there were fewer, but the flag is periodically updated.

A funfact: the starred circle perfectly represents the night sky of November 15, 1889 in Rio de Janeiro, the day in which Independence was proclaimed. The Southern Cross is among the other constellations present. It is the only star above the band and represents the state of Parà.

On the band in the middle of the circle, you will find Brazil's famous motto: order and progress. One of Brazil's very first flags lasted only a few days and looked a lot like the flag of the United States except for its cariocan colors. Today's flag was inspired by the flag of the Brazilian Empire that was once controlled by Portugal.

ARGENTINA

The Argentine flag has three horizontal stripes: sky blue, white and sky blue. At the center you can find the "Sol de Mayo", the sun of May, which symbolizes the historic events of May 25, 1810 when the Viceroy was deposed.

25 MAYO 1810

The flag was created by Manuel Belgrano, who had the difficult task of distinguishing between the independent forces and the Spanish loyalist forces that they were fighting.

Until then, in fact, both sides had used the same colors: red and the yellow.

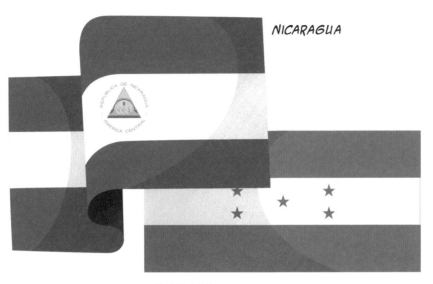

NICARAGUA

HONDURAS

Nine days after drawing the cockade for the army, he also drew the flag. It did not originally have the "Sol de Mayo". In fact, the sun was modelled after the symbol found on Argentinian coins and it was added at a later stage.

Today there are still two valid versions of the national flag: one with the sun and one without.

The Argentine flag served as a model for the creation of the flag of the Federal Republic of Central America, which gave rise to an entire family of flags in that region, including Nicaragua, Honduras and Guatemala.

The Argentines have a curious custom when they lower their flag, as reported in the "Normas Civiles de Tratamiento de la Bandera Nacional".

Once retrieved from the flagpole, the flag is not folded but rolled in a "ball" with the sun well visible to give the impression that the person is holding the "Sol de Mayo" in his hands.

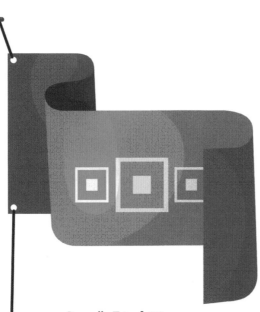

Rossella Trionfetti

Born in 1984, as a child she frequented bookshops and libraries, hungry for illustrated books about animals, showing an early interest in the world of drawing. After her high school certificate in Applied Art, she specialized in the field of illustration and graphics attending a number of courses with professionals of the sector, including the MiMaster of Milano. She currently works as a children's illustrator, also collaborating in the creation of apps and interactive games.

Federico Silvestri

Reading a map, an atlas or globe is the most entertaining activity imaginable for the author of this volume. Having learnt by heart all the capitals of all the countries in the world, he turned his attention to flags.
Half-architect and half-designer, he always dreamed of designing the flag of a fledgling nation. His favourite flags are those of Bahrain, Barbados and Kiribati.

Graphic layout
Maria Cucchi

WSKids
WHITE STAR KIDS

White Star Kids® is a registered trademark property of White Star s.r.l.

© 2018 White Star s.r.l.
Piazzale Luigi Cadorna, 6
20123 Milan, Italy
www.whitestar.it

Translation and Editing: Iceigeo, Milan (Cynthia Koeppe, Caroline Ellen Liou/Simone Gramegna, Elena Rossi)

ISBN 978-88-544-1280-4
1 2 3 4 5 6   22 21 20 19 18

Printed in Croatia